# INVADED BY THE GOD OF THE IMPOSSIBLE

## A Doctor's Adventure in Practical Faith

BY STEPHEN WOOD

ISBN: 978-1-60383-275-5

Published by:
Holy Fire Publishing
717 Old Trolley Rd.
Attn: Suite 6, Publishing Unit #116
Summerville, SC 29485

www.ChristianPublish.com

Printed in the United States of America and the United Kingdom

# Appreciation

For us all, how we begin has bearing on how we finish. I started life with a mother who prayed tenaciously, without which I doubt this story would have been written. Thank you Mom!

My deep appreciation to Jeanne, my treasured wife. She realised it was the Holy Spirit speaking that started this. She fully supported, prayed for and believed in me, caring diligently for our children, and our home during training. We learnt a deep trust in God together. Without her, this story ***certainly*** would not have been written.

There were many close friends during student years in Solihull Christian Fellowship, of which we were then part, who encouraged, prayed and gave. Too many to name, but who God used to bless us. Their contribution is not forgotten.

Our five children, who did not have as much of dad as they needed and would have liked during their early years, but were a vital and necessary part of God's shaping in my life.

To all of you I am deeply grateful. Thanks so much.

Special thanks to my son Jonathan patiently steering me through the complexities of formatting and other computer mysteries! He also designed and produced the cover. Thanks also to Matt Bone who kindly let us use his photograph in the cover design.

Finally, my appreciation to Zelma at Holy Fire Publishing for her advice, support, and bringing it to print.

## CONTENTS

# PREFACE

From my early childhood I have had the privilege of being taught and becoming familiar with the scriptures. I have always found the stories of people and places, and of successes and failures, quite fascinating. They inspired me to expect that following God should be an exciting adventure, even if at times quite a scary one! Sadly, for the first twenty-eight years of my life this was not what I experienced, but then all that changed – quite dramatically!

My intention is to take you with me on a personal journey of what proved to be one of fresh discovery. Times of nail-biting, 'on the edge', walking with God with whom 'all things are possible', just on the basis of believing! I am convinced that God has always planned that each of us are to have an active part in His eternal purposes, but so often our unbelief prevents us from being able to move forward into those purposes. On this journey I trust that you will learn some practical, simple and helpful lessons, as I did, of what it really means to walk by faith, and not by sight.

I have met very few people who, if they are being truly honest, actually love endless routine, the ordinary and mundane, the predicable and expected. After all, much of the massive entertainment industry of today is to enable us, at least for an hour or so, to enter into a make-believe world where unlikely and even 'impossible' co-incidences occur. I believe it is because as humankind we are made to stretch outside the box of what has become routine and normal, and indeed this has always been the seedbed of fresh discovery in every area of life.

While autobiographical, this book is not really about me, but I trust that it will prove to be a powerful testimony of the One, who over about sixty years, I have grown to love and follow, and who I have proven to be totally dependable, loving and faithful. He alone must take the glory. He has purposes beyond our wildest dreams, providing we are prepared to take those first faltering steps! I offer these experiences so that you may build on some of my ceilings, avoid some of my mistakes, and build higher. In this way you can perhaps save yourself from wasting precious years having to re-discover what should be to all of us, basic foundational truths.

# Chapter 1

# A New Perspective

~ 'Could someone please tell me what faith is really all about?' ~

~ Truth, that is never ***outworked,*** will only make us religious, and is unlikely to make us righteous if ***unapplied!*** ~

The scene is that of an examination room. Rows of desks are appropriately placed at fixed distances apart. At each desk is a student, each in a different posture and engaged in different activities. Some gaze out of the window hopefully looking for inspiration. Some are writing passionately and relentlessly like their whole life depended on it – I really struggled with those people! Some looked dejected and decidedly ill, as if a trap door opening beneath them would be a welcome deliverance. At this particular examination I am at one of the desks, about seven back from the front and the fourth row from the right. It is in the Arthur Thompson Hall of the Birmingham Medical School in June 1972. As I write I am picturing it vividly.

Come back there with me for a few moments and read my thoughts, and you will find that I am having, what I know to be, a futile argument with God. He and I have gone into this examination together, and we are seated at the same desk, although of course the invigilators can only see me – which is certainly advantageous because had my Helper been perceived that would have probably been the end of my time as a medical student! Now my gripe is this. God gave me His word prior to this examination that He would help me, and I have to say for the first four questions of this paper, things have gone well. However, I have hit an impasse as I still have to answer a fifth question, and out of the remaining options I cannot find one that I can even start, yet God keeps telling me there is. I keep telling Him there is not, and that He must be mistaken, which I also know is a stupid thing to tell God. I sense Him telling me to look at question one. I have already looked at that hopefully several times and I cannot do it. The ensuing conversation went something like this: 'Why are You telling me I can do that when I know I cannot?' 'Because you can'. 'Wait a minute'. 'That is fine, I have the whole of eternity to wait, but you are running out of time!' 'Yes, I know I am running out of time, but that just does not help me. Look, I have just seen something - yes, you are right, I can do this question' 'At last son, I have been telling you for the last ten minutes that you could.' 'Lord, please let me answer this question!' I write like fury to the finishing bell, just like those candidates I cannot stand!

We both leave the examination room to return many times over during the ensuing years. This was one of many situations that you will read of as you progress through these pages, and of how an ordinary fellow, learnt to listen to, and walk with, an extraordinary God.

We soon learn that words can carry different meanings when shared between people. Sometimes the difference will be slight and insignificant, yet at other times it will be great enough to give a completely false picture of what was meant by the speaker or writer. Over many years in my walk with God I have come to the conviction that 'faith' is definitely one of these words, and it carries a variety of definitions in people's understanding.

When you spend even a relatively short time in the presence of Christians, you are almost certain to hear this word used, and over time we become familiar with hearing it. 'I have faith for that' is often stated. 'Well, I have no faith that that might happen' appears an opposite observation. 'Oh, she lives by faith' might be heard in a conversation concerning someone who does not have regular employment. 'My friend came to faith recently' recounts an enthusiastic soul winner. Even people who would not claim any belief in God at all may be heard to say, 'Oh, I have no faith in that chap.' These conversations will most likely cause us to ask the question, 'Could someone please tell me what faith is really all about?'

Listening to all of the above statements would invariably lead one to conclude that the word must have a variety of definitions, and if so, which one fits where!

After my many years as a church leader, I have come to realise that a very large proportion of Christians who use the word 'faith' freely in their conversation, often have little or no ability to define it when asked, nor have they much understanding of how it can practically be outworked in their lives. On many occasions I have asked a person in conversation what they were actually implying by the word 'faith' in their statement. It sometimes creates interesting, if not amusing situations. 'He is supposed to be a church leader and he is asking ***me*** what I mean by faith? I should have thought every Christian knows what faith is!' Yet on further probing, and a few spluttered clichés about 'belief in God' or 'it is pretty basic surely?' the definitions quickly run out. If I am in a teasing mode, which is not infrequent, I might observe that Satan has a very profound and deep 'belief in God!' However, he is not someone who could be termed in the biblical sense as 'having faith' at all, as we shall later observe.

At this point let me make something clear. I was brought up from birth in a sound Christian environment, both my parents being deeply committed believers in the Christian Brethren movement all of their lives. I was born again and baptised at a relatively early age, and well versed in the scriptures by my later teenage years. At eighteen I was co-leading a young people's bible class, and began preaching soon after. I can vaguely recall even teaching and preaching about 'faith'. Some of my old preaching notes from those days are highly amusing or highly embarrassing, depending on one's perspective! I am glad we did not record our messages in those days – my notes are quite bad enough, let alone tapes gathering dust on people's bookshelves! Had you asked me at that stage of my Christian life to define faith for you, I too would have spluttered and coughed and shown my gross ignorance – and I am ***preaching*** about it! So in seeking to address this problem, I am not coming from some spiritual ivory tower, but as one who was entirely ignorant of the true meaning of faith for many years.

After a very powerful encounter with the Holy Spirit which changed my life radically during my late twenties, and which had been born out of a deep hunger to know the Lord more, I became serious in asking Him what He wanted me to do with my life for the future. He began to reveal to me some startling purposes, such that I began to wish I had never asked! I was a young married man, with a home and two very young children, and a reasonably well paid secure job that I enjoyed. In fact, my question was rhetorical, rather than one for which I was desperate for an answer. I soon realised that the answer that I would have preferred was 'Carry on, son, you are doing fine!'

God began to make it very clear that I was to resign from my employment, and apply to medical school to train as a doctor. I had a hatred of all things academic from my first day at school as a four year old. I have a clear remembrance of it, and its misery only came to an end on that most joyful day when I left grammar school at the age of sixteen! I had achieved only a modest handful of basic UK 'O' levels, equivalent to the more modern British GCSE's! Where would the money come from? How on earth would I cope with a six year course? I knew I did not have the intellectual ability or the qualifications to even get on the course, let alone complete it. What about my wife and children, with our third child on the way now? What about the small and growing church that I was a key leader in at that time, with all the demands of that? 'Lord You must be joking' I thought. I rapidly began to discover that He was not!

At this point in our lives, my wife Jeanne and I began our very first lesson in God's school of faith. This was where we began to learn what faith was actually all about. I could not have defined it for you at that point, but deep down I knew that this was crunch time, and God was going to disciple us in the life of faith that would change us forever. It was almost as if God was saying: 'Now son, you have preached faith, but from here on I will disciple you in living it out. Fasten your seat-belt!'

One of the real issues of modern day Christianity that I perceive, is that we rightly put great value on scripture and biblical truth, but so often fail to apply that truth to our everyday living. We can end up with our minds full to capacity with this truth, but unless it is outworked it will only make us more and more religious. It is unlikely on that basis to make us righteous! We only have to observe the Pharisees in the Gospels to understand that. They were full of scriptural knowledge yet had ended up so deceived that they totally failed to recognize the One that the scriptures pointed to. I am able to speak with some understanding on this, because for many years I would almost go to war for what I perceived was theological correctness, and defend my position to the point of total ungraciousness and anger. The meek and gentle spirit that characterised Jesus, the One I professed to imitate and follow, was entirely absent. It never occurred to me that my actions were completely contradictory. It took several years for me to realise that I did not have to go into battle on God's behalf. He was fully able to defend His own truth without my help! All I achieved was to very badly misrepresent Him.

Our current culture sets great store on rational thought leading to concrete conclusions, and sadly, something of this spirit has insidiously invaded the church over many decades. The possibility of actually experiencing a living God, actively at work in my life, is sadly for many believers almost heresy, and for others only a dream that never seems to come true. Most Christians would agree that God is certainly not a theological idea or concept, but a living person to whom we have ready access through the powerful work of Christ's cross and His shed blood. We are invited to experience our heavenly Father through His many and varied attributes. For instance, we experience His love as we learn to walk and abide in Him. Faith can remain a biblical concept, a theological truth to be analysed, discussed, and admired. But God's clear purpose is that we live in the daily experience of its dynamic power in our lives. There is no other way to live, if we are to enter into all the fullness of life that God intends for each of us to enjoy.

For my wife and I, faith has become a way of life, an unfolding of a little understood truth, in our twenty first century western Christian culture. It is no longer a theory or academic idea to be talked about but never actually lived out. We will begin to delve into it as the journey unfolds further in the next chapters.

# CHAPTER 2

# THE JOURNEY BEGINS

~ I had heard of a few modern day miracles....they certainly had never happened to me. I had no expectation that they ever would! ~

~ Every day is a fresh opportunity in God to discover more of His immense love and plans for us to pursue ~

It was a very significant fact, but completely unknown to me until I began to hear the Lord's fresh direction for my life, that my mother, from my birth, had prayed consistently throughout my childhood and early adult years that I would become a doctor and serve God as a missionary. She always had it in her heart that I would serve the Lord in that capacity abroad. She told my wife to be, when we had become engaged, that this had been her constant prayer, and how disappointed she was that I had not pursued this path. Jeanne never disclosed this fact to me at all at that time.

On leaving school, I began to pursue an engineering career, but through lack of any advanced qualifications I soon realised this would prove a dead end without further academic study. I had no intention of even considering that path! I began to look for other work. My dear mother, avidly scanning the 'situations vacant' column in the local newspaper, found two trainee technician posts at the major city teaching hospital within easy distance of where we lived. I applied for these posts, and landed both jobs! Perhaps she felt that the Lord needed a little help in fulfilling her desires, and this might be a first step! I chose the post in medical physics, and subsequently over some thirteen years was promoted through the various grades to the post of chief technician in the oncology department of the hospital. This led me to work in a team alongside medical professionals, nursing staff, and other technical personnel. While I loved the hospital environment and the work in which I was engaged, any thought of trying to pursue a path into medicine had never even remotely entered my head. While I was engaged in quite complex work in radiation physics, all my learning was through practical involvement rather than books and learnt theory. I planned to keep it that way. One day when relaxing with the medical team over a lunchtime cup of coffee, the subject of conversation became centred around the major changes that were being applied at that time to the medical degree course at the university medical school that was attached to my hospital. It was not a subject that had any interest to me, but as I listened, the main topic being discussed was that the traditional full-scale end of course medical examinations were to be replaced by a form of continual assessment that would follow regularly and consistently throughout the entire medical course. As one of those spontaneous comments which we probably all sometimes make, often just to take some part in the discussion, I remember retorting, 'Oh, even I could cope with a course like that!' It was meant purely as a joke to be forgotten immediately. However, this off-hand comment proved to be a seed that became lodged in my mind. On returning home from work that evening, I entered the house and greeted my wife. My next words to her where 'What would you say if I gave up my job and trained to be a doctor?' Why I said that I have no idea, but I do know that again it was meant entirely as a joke, and was the sort of banter that I would often engage in, and I was prepared that we would just have a laugh together at such a ridiculous notion. To convey better to you the absurdity of this situation, try to imagine the most unlikely and totally unachievable thing that you could ever see yourself doing, and for a bit of fun, telling your closest friend that this is what you proposed to do. You would either expect them to laugh, or be stunned into silence. Instead, Jeanne looked straight at me, and without a glimmer of a smile said 'I feel you should', and turned and carried on with what she was doing. She knew about mother's prayers. In fact, I was stunned, as I realised that she was being serious. I can recall thinking to myself, 'Why on earth did she say that?'

Nothing more passed between us on the matter at that time, but over the following days, I had an increasing sense of unease that there was something brewing inside me that I was not entirely happy about.

I could not get the thought out of my head, however hard I rationalised, about the absurdity of such a proposition. Somehow I needed, for my own peace of mind, to finalise the matter. At least that was as I thought. Accordingly, I decided to go to the medical school faculty office, which was only a two minute walk from the hospital where I worked and onto the university campus. Here I enquired about the possibility of a twenty-eight year old technician, with no advanced qualifications whatsoever, obtaining a place on their course. I could not even claim to having any relative who had studied medicine or even done a course at that university. Back in those days this sometimes helped. The look of utter disdain on the clerk's face said it all. There was no chance of a university place in ***anything***, let alone medicine, and she communicated clearly that I ought to have known better than to waste her time. She firmly announced that I was too old, too late to apply for that year, and totally unqualified. While that was not information that had escaped me, it was what I needed to hear, and I began to leave encouraged. Probably because she felt that she had been a bit tough on what she mistook for an aspiring student, she passed me the faculty booklet which outlined the details of the medical course and the entry requirements. I came away relieved, thinking I had the answer I required.

Casually looking through the booklet later, it seemed to infer that there was a route onto the course via a special examination that gave access to a preliminary course of one extra year of study to bring students up to necessary advanced level standard in the basic sciences. Oh dear, so another trip to my 'friendly' clerk for clarification. This time she stated categorically that this mode of entry was strictly only applicable for overseas students or U.K. students who had achieved other relevant degrees. Again, as an after-thought she gave me an application form. 'They will not let you sit that', she firmly decreed, referring to the academic powers that made those decisions. They did! Reluctantly, I took the examination which to my amazement I passed, although I have no idea how this seeming miracle occurred as I had assessed my performance as a complete disaster!

At this point I am feeling that I am being pushed unwillingly yet inexorably down a narrowing funnel, desperately hoping that at some point very soon this course of events, which was developing into a nightmare, will end with a clear full stop. It did not. It continued with a further series of harrowing interviews, one requiring me to face a board of six university professors, who seemed concerned as to why I wanted to give up my present work to train as a doctor. That was quite difficult, as the honest answer was 'I really have not the slightest idea, and as a matter of fact I do not want a place on your course at all! Stop the train, I want to get off!'

There followed the filling out of the inevitable university clearing (UCCA) forms. These required the candidate to list five choices of university. As I was not prepared to move away from home or could afford to move house, I listed 'Birmingham' five times. They returned the form to me saying I was not allowed to do that, so I sent them another form filled in with 'Birmingham' as my first choice, followed by four blanks. I was not prepared to co-operate in any way! I am hoping that this will finally make it impossible for things to go any further. However, university clearing appeared to give up at that point and accepted the form! Immediately I had completed all the paperwork there was a six week long postal strike when communications went dead. Following the strike I received a letter offering me a place to start the first year of a six year course in medicine at my local university. You could have felled me with a feather! This was the guy who had applied too late, was too old, was totally unqualified, and who had about as much chance of ever getting into medicine as a donkey learning to sing opera!

I had been a child of God for some twenty years at this point. I had read biblical accounts of miracles and believed in them. I had heard of a few modern-day miracles, but they always seemed to be in other lands and happened to people I never knew. They certainly had never happened to me, and I have to confess, up to that point, I had no expectation that they ever would. As I opened that letter, I came face to face with the full realisation that my heavenly Father had a clear purpose and a different direction for my life, and that if I was prepared to discover, pursue, and yield to that, then I could expect to see what was naturally impossible continue to unfold before me. In the words of a good friend of mine, 'If God is who He says He is, then He can do what He says He can do!' I had just witnessed firsthand, that God opens doors that are totally impenetrable as and when He wants to. I had had my very own first miracle.

Up to this point, I realised that this miracle had little to do with me, and that I had exercised no faith whatsoever. All I had done was ask the Lord about my future, and was now back-pedalling as hard as I could as the realisation of what this all meant began to dawn on me. God had heard the repeated prayers of my mother, and her dreams and aspirations, and had not overlooked them. At the time when most students would have begun their medical careers, I was neither remotely interested, nor at a point in my spiritual growth and maturity where I could have embraced that path.

This came to be one of those significant turning points in my Christian life. I had discovered that the God who had up to this time been someone remote and, I felt, not particularly interested in someone like me, was not only interested, but had amazing plans for my life that I could not have believed possible. Not only that, He had opened up a path that, in the world of academia, did not exist. While I had never doubted the reality of God, He had for the first time become 'really' real to me!

I will develop this later, but here He was as the God of today. Up to that point I realised I only knew Him as the God who acted yesterday, and my future expectations were in the God of tomorrow. Sadly, far too many Christians spend their whole lives holding on to this erroneous idea.

The scripture declares Him to be the same 'Yesterday, today and forever'. The profound implications of this are that there is never a moment when God is not willing and eager to take ***you*** up and direct you into His purposes. It always starts from a yielded heart and a desire to actively pursue His will for your life. Instead of settling for testimonies of others from the past, or of just having an expectation for the future, the present can become full of exciting impossibilities for you, as God makes up ways where there are no ways, and opens doors that are impenetrably shut against you. It is not about looking longingly back at what might have been, or looking hopefully into the future for something that might happen. For you and me every day is a fresh opportunity in God to discover more of His immense love and plans for us to pursue.

Over the next chapters I will begin to unpack some of the truths that God taught me as to the meaning and practice of faith in my fresh adventure of discovery.

## CHAPTER 3

# THE NECESSITY OF FAITH

~ 'Without faith it is impossible to please Him''
'Whatever is not from faith is sin' ~

~ Faith is the vital foundation stone on which life as a believer is to be constructed ~

~ Rotting flesh is never pleasing. Only faith emits a pleasant aroma to God! ~

I was now faced with a choice. Take a leap into what appeared to be the scary world of the unknown, or proceed no further, and get on with my life as 'normal'. The first required action and change. It required I determinedly take a step out of my comfort zone. The alternative required nothing on my part whatsoever. I was about to receive my first challenge, and knew that I was going to have to make some discoveries about faith, and how it applied to me and my future.

In looking at the scriptures afresh I found they made two rather astounding statements in reference to faith, which made me sit up and pay attention. This is why I am referring to them at this early point in our exploration.

> ***'And without faith it is impossible to please Him,*** *for he who comes to God must believe that He is, and that He is a rewarder of those who seek Him.'* Hebrews 11:6

> *'The faith which you have, have as your own conviction before God. Happy is he who does not condemn himself in what he approves. But he who doubts is condemned if he eats, because his eating is not from faith; and* ***whatever is not from faith is sin.'*** Romans 14:22-23 (Author's emphasis on both verses)

These statements hardly need us to delve into some massive bible commentary to understand what they are saying. The first scripture makes it abundantly clear that the only way to bring pleasure to our heavenly Father, is by the exercise of faith. This immediately challenges us with the importance of defining and then fully understanding what faith actually is. If we have faith we can certainly bring God pleasure – if we do not have faith, it is equally certain from this verse that we can not! That is clear, so we will avoid developing some complicated theology around it, which all too often we try to do when God's word faces us up with challenging truth!

The second statement is equally clear, if not more arresting, and even disturbing. Here the apostle Paul, within the context of food, makes that all embracive statement, which I will paraphrase: 'Anything that does not originate in, and come out from faith is sin.' Not only does an absence of faith bring the Lord displeasure, it will actually alienate us from Him, because sin cannot dwell in the presence of a Holy God.

At this stage in my new journey of experience with God, I had nothing in me but a desire to bring Him pleasure, and certainly no intention to live the rest of my life out of an unbelieving and consequently sinful source. These scriptures were to form an important part in any of my future decisions.

For a long time I was unable to understand a passage in the letter to the Hebrews concerning faith. In chapter five from verse eleven onwards, the writer is talking about the issue of spiritual immaturity, and challenging his readers to grow up. Instead of needing to be fed with milk like babies, they should have by then grown spiritually so that they could be eating spiritual meat. They needed to be weaned off 'elementary teaching and principles' so that they could advance onto some of the more substantial truths of God. That seemed straightforward enough.
However, in the first three verses of chapter six, the writer is still pursuing this theme. Let me paraphrase those verses into modern vernacular in order to highlight some things:

> *'In the light of what I have just said,* ***let us determine to move on*** *from the very basic foundational truths of our life in Christ.* ***We should not need to keep on going over and over the same basic things*** *– they should be firmly built into our*

*lives by now,* ***and be things we live from.*** *Let me list them. 1. Repentance from fleshly works and 2.* ***Faith*** *toward God. 3. Instruction on baptisms and 4. The laying on of hands. 5. The truth about resurrection and 6. Eternal judgment. With the Lord's help* ***let us grow up and go on!'***

As it was for me at the time, this passage presents a major challenge for the present day people of God. I often hear Christians talking about wanting to hear and learn about the 'deep' things of God, and that is an admirable desire, and was also the intended encouragement of the Hebrews' author. However I do wonder how many of us can say we fully understand and embrace a life of true ongoing repentance and faith rooted entirely in God, live out our baptism of death to the old nature and daily resurrection life in the Holy Spirit, experience and practice the powerful anointing of the laying on of hands, and live resurrection life in the true godly awareness of eternal judgment. Perhaps then we may be ready to move on to some deeper stuff.

I remember being personally very challenged by this list after I had been a Christian for well over twenty years, and coming to realise that I only had a superficial understanding of all of them! Having to face that I was still a baby at twenty 'spiritual' years of age was to say the least, rather challenging. I had better start to grow up!

Again this scripture faces us with the fact that faith towards God is a vital elementary truth on which our lives must be based. It is a foundation stone on which life as a believer is to be constructed. As with natural foundations, no builder can afford to keep re-laying the foundations of the house he is building. They need to be put in properly from the start. So it is with the foundation stone of faith. Far from being a desirable option for the favoured few, it is a basic requirement for every sanctified saint!

I recall when starting my secondary education being faced with the mysteries of algebra and geometry, and staggering through four years of the stuff, never able to really get a grasp of what either were all about. I had the same teacher for all those four years, who constantly mocked us lads that appeared so thick. Then in year eleven, I had another teacher who quickly realised what my problem was. I did not understand the basics of either. Arithmetic was never a problem to me, and as he began to explain the essentially simple fundamental rules of these subjects, I took off like a horse from the starting gate, and passed mathematics 'O' level at over seventy percent. All that in one school year! Without an understanding of the foundation blocks I was totally at sea without a compass. So it is with faith, and why so many believers stagger through life from one crisis to the next. No one has discipled them in these fundamental principles.

Now the fact that faith is one of the essential building blocks of our Christian lives should not come as a surprise to us. The very first thing that opens the door to our entrance into the kingdom of God – is faith! Paul puts it this way:

> *'For by grace you have been saved* ***through faith;*** *and that not of yourselves, it is the gift of God; not as a result of works, that no one should boast.'* Eph.2:8-9. (Author's emphasis)

As a young believer I understood that truth fully, and I learned to use the word 'faith' like all my fellow Christians. I have entered through the door into a new life in Christ by believing the gospel narrative about my sin and the work of Christ on the cross. Now I just get on and live the Christian life – how and by what? This belief that has got me through the door, I think is called faith. Now I better get on and read the bible, and live like all my fellow Christians, doing the best I can to please God by serving Him. In all honesty I cannot say that those years of my life were spent in great joy in the Holy Spirit! It was more like drudgery! What had happened to me was the very thing that Paul is addressing in his letter to the Galatian Christians.

> *'You foolish Galatians, who has bewitched you, before whose eyes Jesus Christ was publicly portrayed as crucified? This is the only thing I want to find out from you: did you receive the Spirit by the works of the Law, or by* ***hearing with faith****? Are you so foolish?* ***Having begun by the Spirit, are you now being perfected by the flesh?'*** Galatians 3:1-3 (Author's emphasis)

Paul is saying: 'Why on earth, having come into the very life of God by being born again of the Spirit through the hearing of faith, which was a powerful miracle, have you now reverted to the very thing that kept you from God in the first place - your fleshly efforts' While this may have great appeal to our ego, as we feel that we must do something of ourselves to gain God's ongoing approval, it actually stinks in the nostrils of the Almighty. Rotting flesh always does. Only faith emits a pleasant aroma to God.

We will discuss that interesting phrase 'the hearing of faith' in a further chapter. Suffice it to say that, like the Galatian Christians, God began to show to me the foolishness of starting my journey with him, by faith, and then essentially saying 'Thanks Lord, I am fine now, I will just get on and live the Christian life as best as I can, and I will see You sometime in glory!' Using the analogy of the builder again, it is like laying the foundations for a house, and then as it is being built, he takes out some of the foundation stones. You would think the guy is crazy. Obviously the house stands or falls on its foundations. So if one of the vital foundation stones on which our lives are built is faith, I came to accept that I was required to know in a great deal more detail of what faith actually is, and how I was to live in it, and by it, on a daily basis. Otherwise my house was in great danger of collapse. Perhaps more accurately, even impossible to build.

## Chapter 4

# Faith Defined

~ I remember feeling that God had placed me on the edge of a precipice with a two thousand meter drop and said 'Jump'! ~

~ 'Faith is the underlying immovable rock-like structure that turns hope into complete certainty, and gives concrete and irrefutable proof that what we are unable to perceive with our natural senses, is in fact real and fully in existence' ~

~ Faith is that which brings hope into certainty ~

Having opened the letter informing me that I had been granted a University place, and having had a little time to get over the shock of its contents mixed with the euphoria of success, I began to have to face the implications of this undeniable miracle that God had performed before my own eyes. It is April, and I now have right of entry into a six year university course in the following October. I will outline some of those implications as I saw them at that time.

It was over ten years since I had studied a text book, and 'studied' was a concept that rarely applied to me unless it was something in which I had an interest. I had long ago put such horrors behind me and a determination never to repeat anything resembling my eleven years in formal education. The prospect of pursuing a first year degree level pre-medical course in physics, chemistry and biology, which was to prove to be above the UK 'A' level standard, was to me an impossible hurdle. Failure was the certain outcome even if I could last the whole of the first year. I also knew that if I resigned from my chief technician post, I would not be able to step back into it if I suffered the humiliation of defeat. I had no paper qualifications, and there were only a handful of centres in the whole of the UK into which my expertise and skills would fit. Finding another post would be virtually impossible, with all the major future problems that that could cause in the way of providing for my family. While I would be eligible for a local authority grant, having never received one in the past, how was that to cover the costs of a married man with a home and children to finance? Expensive textbooks and other equipment were required. Another impossibility that had to be faced and which added to the pressure, was that Jeanne and I had become very involved in a small but growing charismatic home church, that even in its early stages was taking up a significant amount of our time. We were experiencing a fresh life and dynamic in God, and certainly knew we were not to relinquish or even reduce our involvement in that.

I remember feeling at that time that God had placed me on the edge of a precipice with a two thousand meter drop into a ravine and said 'Jump'! I had no parachute or any perceivable means of support, just God's invitation! This was a decision for which I had no previous experience that might instruct or help me. Many of my good Christian friends were fully convinced that this was clearly the will of God and that I should make the jump. After all what further 'proof' did I need? I found myself dryly reminding them that it was not ***they*** who were having to launch into the unknown, and while I appreciated their encouragement, foresight and prophetic revelation, I was the guy required to make the jump, and not them. While they might be able to provide an ambulance at the bottom of the cliff in case of emergency, that was of little comfort to me!

Over the ensuing few weeks, a concise understanding of what faith was really all about began to be shaped within me to the point where I could begin to define it. It is this which I will now share.

In putting together a working definition of faith from scripture, that will help us begin to open up this rich truth, let me make one thing clear. In the context of this journey and study we are talking about ***biblical*** faith, as opposed to the sort of 'faith' that is sometimes used in a rather loose and everyday sense. We might hear someone say 'Oh yes I have every faith in my doctor'. What is meant by this is that the doctor appears to be a skilled and trustworthy individual who has his or her patient's best interests and well-being at heart. He or she will hopefully come to right decisions about their patient where diagnosis and treatment are concerned. However, if pressed, we will have to admit that this doctor is like us, a fallible human being. He or she could fail to diagnose a potentially fatal disease with disastrous consequences. In these circumstances we would find our 'faith' was misplaced. Unfortunately our trusted doctor missed it, and we will most likely find it hard to have 'faith' in him or her ever again.

I have heard people trying to define faith as like sitting on a chair. When presented with a chair, even one with which you are unfamiliar, you will sit down on it. You do not grovel on the floor inspecting the underneath, or pick it up and test the strength of the legs, or check it out for woodworm, or even get someone else heavier than you to sit on it first. You sit down on it without question, thus demonstrating your 'faith' in the chair. Sadly to the cost of some people, this 'faith' can be abruptly terminated, with an indecorous collapse under gravity to the floor! I have experienced that embarrassment, and also had to treat patients who have suffered that awful fate! Let me state very clearly - this is ***not*** the 'faith' we are talking about, as scripture defines it. While it may help to illustrate an aspect of the truth, it falls far short in that the source of godly faith is, of course, God Himself.

For the best biblical definition of faith that I know, we return to the book of Hebrews:

> *' Now faith is the substance of things hoped for, the evidence of things not seen. '* Hebrews 11:1

While a superficial reading of that verse does begin to gives us some vital clues as to what faith is, we need to unpack some of the words if we are to understand the two phrases properly. We will take them one at a time.

Firstly the verse tells us that faith is ***'the substance of things hoped for'.*** The word translated 'substance' (or in some translations 'confidence' or 'assurance') is a word in the Greek which literally means ‘substrata’ or perhaps a little more helpfully - ‘that which comes underneath to give support’

If you want to build a road across open farmland, you do not start by immediately laying tarmac across a ploughed field. You have first to dig down to some firm ground by removing the soft upper soil, and then placing on top of that now exposed firm under-soil, a deep layer of crushed stone or ‘road metal’. After that has been firmly compacted you can begin to put down your various layers of tarmac. Only then will the road be able to carry the constant heavy transport required of it, over the many years that follow. The vital layers of stone under the tarmac is our ‘substance’ in this phrase. While it will not be seen, without it our road will from the outset prove to be unusable and quickly ruined.

In the same manner, if you want to make a road across a river you have to build a structure first to support the road. Tarmac does not float on water! So the bricks, or steel and concrete structure that is essential to support the road surface is our ‘substance’
In that same way faith is the solid underlying guarantee that what we hope for will be realised. Put another way, it is the bridge on which our hope is brought into reality.

There is an interesting interplay between the words ‘hope’ and ‘faith’. I will illustrate it in this way. Suppose I have a very rich aunt, who is worth millions, and I am her favourite nephew – I would be certain do all I could in my power to gain that coveted position! As my aunt is clearly getting older and older, a hope begins to arise in me that I just might get a slice of her fortune when she departs this mortal soil. Certainly in this situation ‘Hope remains eternal in the human breast’. At this point I have nothing whatsoever on which to base my hope. Aunt has never made any statements or indication to me that I can even just transiently lock onto, that can fuel and confirm my hope. It remains a vague possibility – nothing more.

Then one day I am with her, and suddenly she says to me 'Oh, I thought I had better tell you as I am getting older, I have left my whole estate to you when I die. I have had my solicitor draw up my will. It has been witnessed and signed, and here is a copy for you to keep.' Within an instant, my hope has changed from a wistful longing into a certain reality. I now have 'substance' to my hope. I now have a bridge which my road from hope to realisation can cross. I am a happy man! Faith is that which brings hope into certainty.

Secondly we learn that faith is: '***the evidence of things not seen'*** The word translated 'evidence', (or in other translations 'conviction') literally means from the original text 'that by which a thing is proved and tested'.

Consider a geologist with years of experience in oil exploration, equipped with all the latest scientific instruments. He is standing on a piece of desert land proclaiming to a group of prospectors and engineers 'If you drill here, at about three hundred meters depth you will strike oil'. Now at that point there is no evidence whatsoever to the assembled group that there is any oil under the earth where they are standing. They cannot see it. They cannot smell it. They have no external evidence whatsoever that what this guy is saying is true. However because of who he is and his track record, they go to the expense of drilling at that very spot. At three hundred and nineteen meters they strike oil!

We are told that we are surrounded and bombarded constantly by electromagnetic waves being beamed out from transmitters all over the world. I am not aware of them. I cannot see, smell or handle them. I do not know they are there, and I will never know until I am given a device that is able to 'see' them and 'handle' them. I pick up my mobile telephone, and hear my wife's voice clearly speaking to me from another continent, and I immediately have 'the evidence of things not seen'.

In both cases the thing that I doubted because I could not 'see' it, has been proved and tested. I have no further argument to come up with – I am silenced! We must realise that faith is not some will'o'the wisp, indefinable 'something' that we cannot quite get our heads around. In fact it is the most solid thing there is as we shall go on to demonstrate.

From what we have discovered so far, let me propose a working definition of faith from this verse. I suggest you spend some time really thinking this through and letting it become revelation in your spirit:

> ***'Faith is the underlying immovable rock-like structure that turns hope into complete certainty, and gives concrete and irrefutable proof that what we are unable to perceive with our natural senses, is in fact real and fully in existence.'***

You will immediately see the relevance of this definition and perhaps better understand the decision I was faced with. If ever I needed something rock-like and irrefutable it was then. But I still had a further question. Although having sought to define and explore it a little, I now needed to ask where it comes from and how could I get it! The next chapter will explore this.

## CHAPTER 5

# THE ORIGIN OF FAITH

~ *So faith comes from hearing, and hearing by the word of Christ* ~

~ Suddenly the word of God became alive, vibrant, exciting and challenging ~

~ Faith comes and is birthed into our spirits through, and only through, God's living Word ~

It will come as no surprise to us that the origin of faith is God Himself and it only comes from Him. There is only one source where we can confidently find that 'rock-like' structure that is unchangeable, immovable and utterly trustworthy, no matter what is happening and changing around us.

Jesus makes a surprising statement that Mark records in chapter 11:22. which many commentators suggest a more accurate rendering is ***'Have the God-kind of faith.'*** This was in response to Peter's comment on the fate of the fig tree that Jesus had cursed the previous day. The succeeding verses continue the theme of faith that we will come back to. At this point, Jesus is clearly indicating to His followers, that faith is available to them there and then, with no apparent requirement of certain hoops that they had to jump through first, or a long series of lectures. As it turned out they were already on the course, during their daily walk with Jesus, watching and learning as they followed Him.

Paul also makes this clear in Romans in the middle of a discourse on Israel's failure to see the unseen.

> *'So faith comes from hearing, and hearing by the word of Christ.'* Rom.10:17

Not only does faith originate from God, but this verse states ***how*** it can be received. It comes from listening to that which God is saying. Here I want to make a very important point. Paul does not say faith comes by hearing what God ***might have said***, or for that matter what God ***maybe will say***, but rather from hearing that which God ***is saying***. It does not say that faith comes by having heard. In chapter 2 I made the point that with God, things are always in the present. There is an immediacy about the word of God – a 'nowness' (if I am permitted to create a new word), a vibrancy. It has the very eternal life of God in it.

In my early Christian experience, I came to believe that God never said anything in the here and now. All that God had to say, He had already said. I was told that we had the bible which was all we needed. That was God's word, inspired by the Holy Spirit, and when the full canon of scripture was finally decided in the third century A.D., then God had nothing else to say and fell silent. I used to ask, 'Well, how can I know the will of God for my life?', and I was told that it would be in the bible. I did not find that very helpful as I quite liked the idea on leaving school of becoming a chemical engineer, and I did not see any references to chemical engineers in my concordance, so that job was out! If God was not talking now, and faith only came by hearing what God was saying, how was I going to obtain it? If God was no longer speaking, then all the listening in the world would be of no help.

Then, as I mentioned earlier, in my later twenties I came into a powerful encounter with the Holy Spirit that radically changed me. Suddenly the word of God became alive, vibrant, exciting and challenging. I began to hear God speaking to me as I read the scriptures, as I talked with other believers, as I prayed, as I listened to the scripture being shared and expounded by others. I began to hear Him speaking to my inner spirit. I began to learn to hear the voice of God on the inside of me. Suddenly I came to realise that God had not absented Himself from engagement with His children. I was not left with an instruction manual that apparently failed to cover the many practical aspects of my life about which I required guidance, precious as the scriptures were. Jesus had in fact sent the Holy Spirit to come and remain with me, as He had promised, and that He was here today to lead me into all truth. The full truth of all that the Father is saying right now to me today.

Yes, my early teachers were right. The scriptures are the inspired word of God. Anything that contravenes them cannot be God's voice. That is so important to know, and I am so deeply grateful for those who taught me to read, learn, study and honour the scriptures. But on the other hand, No, they were not right, because God ***is*** speaking today, and if I will take the time and trouble to listen properly, I will hear His voice in a whole variety of ways. Through the scriptures, through people, circumstances, dreams, visions, and any other way God might choose. I just have to keep my receiver switched on to all the appropriate wavebands.

There are two Greek words in the New Testament that appear translated as 'word' - ***logos*** and ***rhema.*** The first - *logos* - is often used in reference to the recorded word of God as in the bible. Here we find instruction and principles that we can learn and obey, and find that they will bring life and vitality to us. The scripture has an inherent life within it which is not surprising considering it has been inspired by the Holy Spirit working powerfully in the various writers. It is important to read it regularly, study it, and seek the Holy Spirit's help to bring revelation from it to you.
The second - *rhema* - is that word which is being spoken now, and is fresh and immediate. On many occasions it is as if God has taken a fluorescent highlighter pen and underlined a biblical verse, phrase or truth, as I have been reading the scriptures, or has reminded me of a passage as I have been praying or just going about my daily duties. It may be through a prophetic word spoken over me, or through a dream or vision.

Let me make something clear here. I do refute the dangerous practice of always pursuing so called rhema words without any checks, balances and reference to what God has already said in His written word. 'Rhema' words that seem to be giving significant directions into my life need weighing and checking out with others. God will confirm such things to our fellow believers and leaders as well, enabling us to move forward in security. The neglect in recent years of a thorough knowledge of the scriptures in so many, has brought untold problems, deception and shipwreck to the body of Christ, by people just launching out on what they have believed is a 'now' word from God, and subsequent events showed that clearly it was not.

Faith comes by hearing what God is saying. God's voice and faith seems to me to be one and the same thing, or at least inextricably linked. God just speaks and what He has spoken out just happens. There are no discussions or arguments.

*'Then God said, 'Let there be light'; and there was light'.* Gen.1:3.

There was no decision on the part of light as to whether to be a waveform or a particle. At one point it does not exist, God speaks, and there it is! Light itself, so common to us all that we hardly ever think about it, is still proving a mystery to scientists who continue to discuss and share theories. They seem little nearer truly understanding its mysteries than they ever did.

The originator of faith, is speaking, and what He is saying into our lives becomes faith within us, as we hear and obey His 'now' word. Put another way, faith comes and is birthed into our spirits through, and only through, God's living word. There can be no other source from which faith is generated.

When I was facing what appeared at the time to be my momentous decision to jump off my virtual cliff edge or not, I quickly concluded that adding up the 'fors' and 'againsts', analysing the risks, and generally losing sleep and becoming irritable was not helping me, nor was it giving me the answers that I needed. What I required was a word from God that would generate faith within me. The words from friends, encouraging as they were, were not achieving that.

Encouragement from my wife Jeanne, who by now had told me of my mother's constant prayers, was still not adequate. I had one or two prophetic words during those weeks of decision which were also a blessing. But, what I needed was that conviction in my own spirit, where I knew without a shadow of doubt that ***God*** was saying 'Jump!' I needed that living 'now' rhema word.

I recall the occasion when it came. I had put off making the final decision to the very last day when I could give my current employer the required one month's notice prior to accepting my place at the university and leaving my paid work. As I drove to work on that morning, I felt apprehensive, knowing that the all-important letter was to be written and delivered that day. There was no further room for manoeuvre, turning back, or escaping that decision any longer. I sat at my desk with paper and pen in hand. I recall sending up one of those '11.59' prayers, that consist mostly of 'Oh God, Oh God, Oh God....!' and little else. The precipice and chasm appeared even more foreboding. The impossibility appeared even more impossible. Suddenly what I can only describe as a 'heavy peace' entered my office, which I now know was the manifest presence of God. I heard no booming voice, or even a still small one. I was not reminded of any scripture, nor did I have any vision. What I did have was the silence and 'weight' of His presence that brought complete peace to my weeks of indecision, and spoke louder than any human voice. I knew that my Father was saying, 'This is the way, walk in it.' At that point I had the 'rock-like substance' or substrata of God's word underneath me, and the irrefutable proof of what I could not possibly see and understand in my natural mind. With that firmly inside me, I took my pen and literally signed away my career, and all that I had worked for to that point. This was the beginning of a crazy roller-coaster ride with God who every time proved true to His word and His promises. I had finally jumped off the edge! I had no parachute, but I knew I had His word, which was as reliable as the One who had spoken it. Remember, parachutes fail – God does not!

It may appear a contradiction in terms to speak of God's peace and presence as a 'voice', but when you suddenly experience His manifest Presence, all your questions vanish, and in your spirit you just know His will. For consistency I still prefer to call that God's voice, as the effect is identical to that of hearing actual words.

# Chapter 6

# Examples of Faith

~ (Abraham) grew strong in faith, giving glory to God, and being fully assured that what He had promised, He was able also to perform ~

~ David was not a man of faith of the occasional moment, but of the constant abiding ~

~ Knowing that God is All-Wise as a theological concept is of no help whatsoever. We have to learn how to **draw** on that truth! ~

We will now consider some examples from scripture to see faith practically worked out in the lives of real flesh and blood characters. My mind goes go straight to Abraham, who the scripture describes as 'our father in faith'. In spite of his mistakes, which folks sometimes seem to major on, probably to cover their own frailty, Abraham was a remarkable man in his solid trust and obedience to God. Born into an entirely pagan society in Ur, a very modern and advanced city in its day, the only 'gods' he would have been brought up to worship would have been idols created by other men with all their demonic associations. Hardly the best of an environment for a life of faith!

According to Acts 7, Abraham, while he lived in Ur, had a life changing encounter with the 'God of Glory', and from then on he made a decision to hear and obey what God was saying to him.
The first bombshell that God delivered was that he must leave the comforts of the city in which he was dwelling, including his wider family and friends, and just go. In these situations I like to imagine the conversation Abraham might have had with the Lord. 'Go where Lord?' 'Just go, Abraham. Do not worry, I will give you the necessary directions as you set out!' 'Well Lord, let us have a heart to heart discussion about this. I am not sure Sarah will agree, and in fact I am not so sure myself. Perhaps I need to sleep on this for a while – a week - a month – a year or two. In fact it would help if you could give me a clue as to where this is all leading and I could book some advance accommodation' 'No Abraham, it is now, and it is a tent – that is all you will need'.

I wonder how you and I might have responded to that? What is amazing is that Abraham with no further ado, as far as we are told, takes off into no-man's land, and into an incredible adventure for the rest of his life with God. Genesis records this in some detail for us. Is this guy out of his mind, because if he is there is no point in discussing him further, or could it just be that this is to be normal 'Christian' living, and we have got things seriously wrong? In fact could ***we*** be crazy living a different way?

Scripture constantly holds Abraham up as an example, that the nation of Israel were to emulate, but sadly failed to do. The new testament church was likewise to be modelled on that same example. As 'sons of Abraham' by faith, we are not given any option either if we are to bring joy to our heavenly Father and keep from sinning against Him.

Throughout the life of Abraham there are many instances of his hearing the word of God to him, and his obeying it. The classic occasion was over the birth of Isaac following the promise of God that he and Sarah would have a child to fulfil the Lord's covenant to them. Abraham would become the father of many nations, and his offspring would be as countless as the stars in the sky at night. Most of you will know the story with its various twists and turns. Paul takes up the story in his letter to the Romans, and chapter four is more or less entirely devoted to Abraham. It deserves a careful read when considering the subject of faith. Consider for a moment this particular passage as an example.

> *'And without becoming weak in faith he (Abraham) contemplated his own body, now as good as dead since he was about a hundred years old, and the deadness of Sarah's womb; yet, with respect to the promise of God, he did not waver in unbelief, but grew strong in faith, giving glory to God, and being fully assured that what He had promised, He*

> *was able also to perform.'* Romans 4:19-21. (Author's parenthesis)

God had spoken a promise into Abraham's life. It was a living word that had inherent in it, the power to perform what appeared to be naturally impossible. Abraham simply believed it, because God had said it. He had learned that God's word was creative. The same word of God that created the world out of nothing, would create the fulfilment of that promise in both Abraham's and Sarah's dead reproductive systems. Abraham was no fool. He had carefully considered the whole issue - his body and Sarah's body. He knew the score. Nil nil! But he did not waver in questioning God's promise, and fall into unbelief. Instead his convictions grew stronger and stronger, and he begins to praise and glorify God each day, having no doubt whatsoever that this was no problem to God who had promised it. It is worth observing that Abraham was first given the promise when he was seventy five years old, and he was about one hundred when Isaac was born. That was a twenty five year wait! I have known God give promises to people, and when they have not come about in three or four minutes they quit! There is a verse in the letter to the Hebrews that I sometimes remind myself in relation to this:

> *'....that you may not be sluggish, but imitators of those who through faith* ***and patience*** *inherit the promises.'* Hebrews 6:12 (Author's emphasis)

It is the 'patience' bit that we would rather not have to face!

The story of David's victory over the Philistine giant Goliath, in 1 Samuel 17, is another example of faith. I have purposely selected this, because there is no written account of David having a clear word from God to go and kill Goliath. From the story, David is sent with provisions for his brothers who are with King Saul and the Israelite army supposedly fighting the Philistines. As David approaches the camp he hears the taunts of this giant of a man Goliath, and immediately indignation rises up inside him. He is all there with sleeves rolled up ready to go and take him out. If faith comes by hearing the 'now' word from God, what are you doing David? You really need to go and have a time of prayer and get the word of the Lord on this one, or you are in for a fall in a big way!

So is this David in presumption, hoping that God will back him up if he misses the mark? I do not think so. We know that David was a 'man after God's own heart'. Even as a young man he was intimate with God. He knew God deeply through daily fellowship. He was in touch with what God was saying on a more or less constant basis. I say more or less, because at the time of his sad adultery and murder of Bathsheba's husband, David must have been temporarily outside his normal place in God, otherwise he would never have committed those gross sins. David expresses his deep honour and regard for the word of God time and time again in the Psalms. I give the following as an example:

> *'Your word I have treasured in my heart, that I may not sin against You'.* Psalm 119:11.

David lived in that place of intimacy, and with a freshness and a hearing ear to the voice of God in his everyday life. As he came that day into the battle scene, his was not the presumption and arrogance of youth or merely human response. A divine anger arose in his spirit as he heard the name of his closest friend, God Himself, being reviled by a godless Philistine. I am quite sure he heard the voice of God in his spirit which undergirded his call to action. David was not a man of faith of the occasional moment, but of constant abiding. Therein lies another challenge for us today. Instead of developing a close friendship with God, seeking to walk with Him on a daily basis, we live life in relative isolation from Him, fuelled by the hectic pace of our everyday lives. We may be regular attenders at church meetings, but that can never replace a life lived in the presence of God.

When some crisis hits our lives we want an immediate answer from the Lord. No wonder many find difficulty in obtaining it. The life of David teaches us the necessity of living close to the Father, if we are to build lives that truly are lived out of faith, and please Him. We need to live in the familiar territory of the presence of the Lord. I meet many people these days who are embracing this wonderful privilege and are learning to live their lives out from that divine centre.

I myself had to learn this lesson very quickly as I commenced the first year of my medical course. I had always had an interest in science, and these were the only subjects I had any real success in at school. However, the level and complexity of the subjects that I was now being required to study was far above anything that I had ever done previously. Within the first two or three weeks of my new adventure I felt totally out of my depth and sinking fast. I knew that God was taking me on a journey, and that He was the bedrock beneath me – the 'substance of things not seen' – and that He knew the subject matter with which I was struggling! Organic Chemistry was not a problem to the Lord. He put it all together in the first place, vital as it is to our physical living, and He maintains its complex functioning!
I would often come out of lectures dazed, having sat for some forty five minutes hardly understanding the words, let alone the concepts being espoused. At times I would question what I was doing in this environment. I felt like a fish out of water – almost an interloper who had got there by false pretences. My fellow students all appeared to be absorbing and understanding every word, and while I later discovered this was far from true, it would only add to my sense of misplacement. I would go home and struggle for hours with atomic theory or thermodynamics, knowing these things would not really be of great use when removing someone's appendix, or prescribing medication for a diabetic!

I had no resource within myself, which was the powerful lesson the Lord was teaching me. In the past I had been very resourceful, having the ability to do most things. From a child I was always inquisitive as to how and why things worked. I recall managing to undo all the screws in an old pocket watch belonging to my father, and seeing it almost literally explode as the fully coiled spring inside was suddenly released. The ensuing interview with my dad did not go well from my viewpoint! I did not have a clue how to put all this back together again and neither did my dad. By the time I went to medical school, there was little to which I could not turn my hand. I added to my grant in the initial years by electrical rewiring of houses, plumbing, and servicing and repairing motor vehicles in my driveway. Our neighbours at that time were very kind and tolerant knowing the reason for all this activity.

These resources however, were of no direct help with my studies, and so I was constantly leaning into God for His wisdom, support, and addition to my lacking intellect. Knowing that God was all-wise as a theological concept or even a firm belief was of no help whatsoever. I had to learn how to draw on that truth, if I was going to make it through.

Two examples of the way in which God gave me His assistance come to mind. One day, after I was a few weeks into the course, a neighbour living a couple of houses away, who I knew very little about, came round to my home asking if he could borrow a certain tool. He had heard of my new venture, and asked me how things were going. I told him I was really struggling with some of the general chemistry and physics. He immediately responded by telling me that he was a college lecturer in chemistry and physics, and loved teaching and would be only too willing to help me if I required it. I was round at his home the following night, and many times during that first year. He proved to be an exceedingly good and patient teacher - he needed to be! - and proved to be an invaluable and free provision of God for that critical year. He moved house and left the area soon after, but I believe the Lord had him there exactly on time to help me when I needed it.

Another instance occurred during my end of first year examinations. I had experienced a real breakthrough in chemistry, and had just taken the examination in the subject, and was on an emotional 'high'. Had I been asked to write my own examination paper, I do not think I could have done a better job than the examiners. It was tailor made for me, and I knew even before I had put a pen to paper I had passed it. However, my elation was to prove short-lived as having put about seventy percent of all my effort into this, I was faced now with the Physics paper, with only ten days to revise and pull things together for that next examination. I looked at my vast pile of lecture notes, and decided there and then that this was the end. I was finished. 'Lord, You have delivered me from Egypt and slain all my enemies in the sea, but now three days later I am dying of thirst and the water in this oasis is undrinkable'. Like Israel, I knew what it felt like, and had quickly forgotten the God of the 'Red Sea' chemistry! Miracles define God's ***acts*** for you, but they do not always teach you about God's ***ways***.

I went into fitful sleep, and I shall never forget the feeling of complete dejection and despair. The following morning, before I went off to university (as I lived and worked from home), a letter was delivered. I immediately recognized the hand-writing. It was that of my mother. On a scrap of paper torn out of an exercise book she had written the following words: 'I feel the Lord wants me to send you this scripture - *For I am the Lord Thy God, will hold thy right hand, saying unto thee, fear not; I will help thee'*. Isaiah 41 verse 13.' (You can tell my mother used the King James Version.)

The timing of this letter was remarkable as my mother living 160 miles away, would have had no idea about the evening and night I had just gone through. Only my heavenly Father and my wife knew. The more remarkable thing was that my mother had never ever taken such action before, at least certainly not for me. Very godly lady as she was, she had never, as far as I had been aware, moved in the prophetic, or would ever presume to say to anyone, 'I feel the Lord is saying this to you'. She had never previously sent me such a letter, and never sent me one of this nature at any time afterwards.

If only I could convey in writing the effect that this simple note had on me. I knew without a shadow of doubt that this was an invasion of the word of God into my distraught situation. I knew that those words were sent directly to me by the Lord as if He had personally come into my room and had spoken them into my ear. I recall fully embracing those words, thanking and praising God for His loving-kindness, the obedience of my mother in working completely outside her comfort zone, and His promise to hold my right hand through this next hurdle. Those words generated a certainty of hope and a conviction of success as yet unseen. I turned to my studies with renewed vigour, refreshed and full of true faith that emanated from that 'logos' and 'rhema' word.

One of many evidences of the Lord holding my right hand occurred as I was working for this next examination. There was a part of the physics course that for some reason I found very hard to grasp, and one of the compulsory examination questions had to be answered from this subject. I had about thirty possible topics to choose from for that question, and I can remember almost word for word what I said to the Lord over the issue. 'Lord, You know I have a major struggle understanding Optical Physics. You also know I no not have the time to spend hours trying to get to grips with all this. Please would You give me one of the questions for this part of the paper?' I sat in my chair with pen and paper, and said to the Lord. 'Lord I am going to write down on this paper the first subject that comes into my head, and that will be the subject, and the only subject that I will study in Optics!'

I sat back in the chair, closed my eyes, and within seconds into my mind came the thought 'Newton's rings', so I wrote it down. I knew what Newton's rings were from my interest in photography. For my non-scientist readers, an example of them is the visual phenomenon that occurs when the sun shines on water on which there is a layer of oil, and you will often observe the rings of the colours of the rainbow reflected back at you. You may see them on a wet road where vehicles have been standing. The scientific term for these are diffraction patterns.

I had in my possession the examination papers from the previous seven years, so I naturally searched them to see how many times this subject had previously occurred. The answer was challenging – never! Now what do I do – panic? What I did do was simply say to the Lord, 'You have said You will hold my right hand and lead me, thank You for Your leading in this. I put my full confidence in Your living word to me.'

I studied the physics behind this phenomenon and learned it thoroughly, but nothing else in optics – I did not have time. On the day of the examination I could not help turning straight to the optics section of the paper and there was the question: 'Derive from basic principles the formula for Newton's rings, and work out the following example'. Do you think that might have helped me forward for the remainder of the examination paper? Another co-incidence?

One of the humorous sides to all this was that when sharing these details with my Christian friends, who were involved with us and prayed regularly, several laughingly responded with the observation that when I qualified as a doctor they would not want to be one of my patients as I cheated in examinations! I can assure you that this was not the path I enjoyed in the majority of examinations and assessments, but occasionally when my back was firmly against the wall, the Lord did give me some helpful insights. However, I always knew that I had to give my very best, and He would make up for my inadequacies. That year, I learned to walk a little closer to Him, and to hear His voice a little clearer.

# CHAPTER 7

# DISCIPLED INTO FAITH

~ Jesus was telling His disciples that all they had to do was tell the storm to shut up, instead of baling faster! ~

~ Storms usually come in the middle of the lake. The enemy will challenge your walk of faith when you are at your most vulnerable ~

~ It is vital we learn to distinguish between what may be circumstantially true, and what is THE TRUTH ~

Throughout His life, Jesus was constantly teaching His disciples lessons in faith. I love these scenes, representing as they do so aptly, my walk of faith and the lessons I am still learning. I always attempt get into these scenes, and try and put myself in the place of the disciples. I am quite sure that I would have been no better than they were, as time and time again, they had to bear the Master's rebuke over their lack of faith. Until I began to understand the truth about faith and how it needed to operate in my life, I used to think how hard the Lord appeared to be in His rebukes.

As an example let us look at the storm on the lake. Here are the disciples, hardened experienced fishermen on the Sea of Galilee that they knew intimately, panicking, being fully aware that their boat is heading for the bottom because of a sudden and violent storm. Jesus is asleep in the boat, apparently totally oblivious to their plight. Surely they are fully justified, to shake Him out of His sleep, accusing him of not apparently being too bothered that they are seconds away from a watery grave! Jesus stands up and simply tells the storm to shut up, then proceeds to rebuke the disciples for their lack of faith – I ask you! Is Jesus annoyed with them for His rude awakening? Not at all, but knowing they are going to have to learn the lessons of faith if they are to survive the future years that face them when He has gone, He cannot let them off the hook.

If we go back to the beginning of the story, we find that Jesus, who always did what His Father was doing, was going over to the other side of the lake for a confrontation with Legion, the demon possessed man. The living 'now' word to the disciples that morning was 'We are going over to the other side of the lake.' Now if faith comes by hearing the word of God, that was all the disciples required to get them across the lake. The fact that the enemy understandably tried to abort the whole operation should have been entirely incidental and irrelevant. The reason Jesus was asleep was probably because He was tired! I have heard all different 'spiritual' reasons given for this, but never that one. He was after all a man. The reason He could sleep through the storm was because He was totally at rest in the will of His Father, and as such lived in total peace and rest of heart. In the finite time it was taking to get across the lake He could enjoy some refreshing sleep. You see Jesus was not bothered whether they went across on the bottom of the lake like fishes, six feet above the lake like birds, or actually on it in the boat, or a combination of all three! That was not the issue. The word of God was 'We are going over to the other side', so however impossible the prince of darkness may try and make it, it will happen anyway, because faith is the substance of things hoped for, the evidence of things not seen. Jesus was pointing out to His disciples that all they had to do was tell the elements to be quiet, instead of baling faster. Obviously any faith they started with had got baled out with the water!

A repeated observation I have made in my own life, as well as in the lives of others, is that in our walk of faith on the word of God, the storms always come in the middle of the lake. It did not come before they set out, nor did it come when they had arrived. Satan will nearly always challenge your walk of faith exactly when you are at your most vulnerable. It is also worth noting that frantic baling - human ideas - will not bring about the result that leaning fully on God's word to you will! I have had to learn the hard way, that God does not need my assistance to bring His word to pass in my life. The birth of Ishmael was not one of Abraham and Sarah's sharpest ideas.

During my medical course I found myself struggling with one particular subject having failed three assessments in succession. An essay in the same subject, which would also be part of my overall assessment, was not going at all well either. The essay choice to which I felt the Lord had directed me appeared to be proving a disaster, with a most unhelpful tutor and many of the reference books missing or out on loan from the library. I began to pursue another essay subject, and that was proving even worse! I was faced with what appeared to be certain failure in that part of the course. This would entail a viva voce examination in the subject, which I was convinced I would fail, requiring the retake of an examination in the subject after the summer vacation. I fully expected that I would fail that too, which would result in a retake of the whole year with no financial grant to cover it.

You can see I was not moving in faith in that particular subject! I knew I had lost my peace and confidence in the word of the Lord that He had made to me at the start of the year. Without dressing it up, I had sunk into total unbelief. Please do not tell me 'without faith it is impossible to please God' or 'that which is not of faith is sin'. That sort of ministry is not going to help me right now – so back off and let me enjoy a moan, a grumble and a sulk! I have to tell you that Father in all His grace, mercy and kindness did not allow me to do that. Satan is attacking me mid-term, but the Lord spoke into my spirit. 'So what if you fail son? I love you anyway. Are you more concerned about your glory than Mine, - how ***you*** will look with your fellow students if you have to retake? What was My word to you?'

I am now in repentant mode, and suddenly the whole thing lifted, and I hear myself saying, 'Even if I have to take a viva voce examination or a resit, Lord I trust Your word with all my heart. You have set me on this course and You will finish it, because Your word and Your glory is at stake here. What You have said to me will surely come to pass'. Suddenly I am alive again and totally unconcerned about the future. It may be stormy right now, but we will get to the other side.

A few days after that encounter, I was accosted by a fellow medical student, who having seen the latest examination results before I had had the opportunity, asked me in mock rage and tongue in cheek what on earth S J T Wood was doing having the audacity to ***pass*** a pathology examination! This really had to stop! We had a good laugh, and I often sense the pleasure and smile of my heavenly Father at these times too. I asked the Lord for forgiveness for my lack of faith in changing to another essay subject, and returned to the one which the Lord had directed me to do in the first place. Not surprisingly it all began to fall into place as I brought the difficult issues to Him.

At the end of that pathology course, when the final results for that subject were posted, I received a 'B' grade, which was a good pass! I had received a double 'A' grade for my essay – only two others in the whole year of one hundred and sixty students attained that, and those of course were girls – they always did work much harder than us lads! I am quite sure to this day that my essay was not of the calibre that deserved that top mark. I suspect the tutor who marked it was reading my words with some 'angelic adjustment'! I was also unaware that all my previous three failed assessments had missed the 'C' grade pass level by only a couple of marks. The final aggregate was more than just satisfactory. Did I learn further lessons during that particular course about 'on the ground' faith? Did I learn that from a sermon? Most times we learn the lessons of faith like Jesus' disciples had to – in the cut and thrust of everyday life and its circumstances.

My other example from the life of the disciples comes from the occasion when Peter walks on the water recorded in Matt.14:22-33. Jesus comes to the disciples who were crossing the lake in a boat on a dark, stormy night, walking on the water no less! After the disciples got over the shock of thinking he was a ghost, Peter decides that he would like to have a go at this rather novel phenomenon. It is worth noting that Jesus walking on the water was not meeting anyone's need.

It was however about to teach the disciples a very important lesson about faith.

'Ask me to come to You on the water, Jesus' Peter calls out. Jesus replies ***'Come!'*** That one word was ***the*** word of truth. It was the living word of God for that situation and Peter could stake his life on it. He was in reality walking on the word of Jesus by faith, not, as he might have supposed the Sea of Galilee. It is worth noting that Peter was the only disciple to get out of the boat and 'have a go', while the rest of the disciples stayed in the security of the boat and unbelief. They never did have the fun of walking on water as far as we know! It is of course possible that the others even chided Peter for his bravado. Sometimes it takes real guts to launch out into unknown realms with God, and too often your fellow disciples will not always join you or encourage you. Sometimes they may even mock you.

What happens next is an equally vital part of the scenario. Peter suddenly realises the craziness of what he is doing, and he takes his eyes off Jesus who has given him the word - Jesus, who ***was*** the word of God made man - and he begins to sink! Why? Because he begins to look at the circumstances around him, and he sees the waves and the wind, and the impossibility of what he is doing. Now bear in mind all that he was now seeing was ***TRUE!*** It ***was*** windy. There ***were*** massive waves, and what is more it ***is*** quite impossible to walk on water! But he has dropped back into the natural realm. He is now believing that which is circumstantially true, rather than ***THE TRUTH!*** His active faith in the word of Jesus to 'Come', was replaced by unbelief in what he saw with his natural eyes - and it was all over. Peter, as he is about to go under yells for help. Jesus pulls him up, and now standing holding him there says 'O you of little faith, why did you doubt!' Peter you were doing so well.

This was a key component as God discipled me throughout my medical course. In the natural realm I was unqualified to even begin on all counts, and as the course proceeded even more natural hurdles presented themselves. Anyone could have made a very sound argument at any stage that I was completely out of my depth, and it would have been entirely true. However, I knew it was not ***the truth***, because God had called me and given me His word, and I came to learn to walk on that alone. When I forgot, the enemy would soon suggest that all the recent successes and apparent miracles were just coincidences, and I soon began to sink! These are the times when there is the need to focus firmly back on the truth of what God has stated and promised.

Walking on God's word, is usually an exhilarating, if not sometimes a scary experience. Nevertheless while it may defy earthly logic, it is the way that Father invites us to live. What we usually term the supernatural, becomes increasingly 'natural' to us. We find the freedom from earthly constraints that Jesus promised His followers:

> *'Jesus therefore was saying to those Jews who had believed Him, 'If you abide in My word, then you are truly disciples of Mine; and you shall know the truth, and the truth shall make you free.'* John 8: 31- 32.

The man and woman of faith will walk on the solid rock of what God has spoken, regardless of what is apparently under their feet. God would teach us that the realm of the Spirit, of that which is eternal, is the only place where we can reliably place our full confidence. It is sad when we give more credence and trust in what scripture describes as 'this world which is passing away' than we do the everlasting word of Almighty God, the Creator and Sustainer of ***all*** things.

# Chapter 8

# Faith and Hope

~ In seeking to understand faith, let us not confuse it with hope ~

~ When God speaks His word into my hope, then faith arises ~

~ Let us have the humility and wisdom to admit it openly when we have made a mistake. It disarms the enemy! ~

We are beginning to build up a picture of what faith is and how it operates. Many times I have been in conversations with Christians, and they have said to me something like 'Oh, I am in faith for a new job in the next few weeks'. 'Wonderful' I am likely to say. 'What word or promises has God given you about that?' Their faces display a puzzled expression. 'Well, I just believe it is going to happen'. My likely response is 'Yes, well great, but what makes you so sure?' 'Well, I've been asking God for a new job, and so I am really in faith for one. After all you are always preaching about God's desire to bless us!' Now please understand that I am not in any way against believers pressing into God for His blessing and progress in their lives. That is not what I am addressing here. However, in this conversation can you see what I am after, and not getting? It would appear that these folks do not have any living Word from God, that can underpin their hope, or bring certainty to what they as yet do not see. I would suggest that these people are not 'in faith' although they appear to think they are, but still only in the realm of hope.

I remember many years a go, a couple in our church making a public announcement one Sunday morning as a sort of 'faith' testimony, that God was going to provide them with a new car, and they gave the make, the model and the colour, that they were 'believing for'. Further enquiry revealed that they had recently heard an address in which it was stated that if you desired something from the Lord you had to ask very specifically for what you wanted, declare to all and sundry what your 'faith goal' was, receive it 'by faith', and then confess every day that it was already yours. I had no major issue with those basic principles, but a vital ingredient was missing. They had received no living word from God on the matter. They were receiving it 'by faith' on the basis of the preaching alone. Any further discussion on the matter was closed, leaving enquirers with the feeling that they were unbelieving infidels, and best not associated with, lest 'our faith' be tarnished. Sad to say, no new car of any description ever arrived over the next two years, by which time the model requested had ceased production. The couple eventually walked away from God, bitter and disillusioned. When Christian friends sought to contact them later they were very still bitter and refused any friendship or encouragement. In fairness, I have no reason to doubt that the preaching that they heard was good and wholesome, but I suspect that they heard only the bits they wanted to hear from the ministry given, and took them out of the context of the whole message. If their 'faith' was in their perception of a preacher's instructions, however good they were, it was not faith at all, rather a personal hope, as they desperately required a new vehicle!

This precious couple, who I knew well, were sincere and were wanting to push some boundaries in their pursuit of God and in the area of faith. I firmly believe that the Lord loves that spirit which seeks to press beyond the familiar and well recognized paths that all too often can become our prison. However I would like to add a word of caution out of this scenario. This couple would receive no accountability outside of themselves. They had not shared, discussed, or prayed over their thoughts or new found 'theology of faith' with any of their Christian friends or those perhaps more spiritually mature than themselves in the church to which they were joined. I know some might interpret this as control – but I have personally discovered that it is wisdom, and many times the route to freedom. When I was seventeen I knew everything there was to know, and my father was really ignorant for his age. By the time I was twenty-seven, I had discovered that I knew very little, and my father was well worth consulting on matters. He had suddenly appeared very wise, and was not as ignorant as I had supposed!

I would suggest that it is the same in the family of God. A wise man or woman will always draw on those who have walked the same road, but for a little longer, even though sometimes in the end we have to pursue the convictions that we believe God is placing within us. If we are part of the body of Christ, and as Paul states 'members one of another', it seems to me foolish to operate as a little cell totally independent of those around us, to whom God has joined us. Just as each cell in the body is sustained by the immediate environment around it, so this is true of the body of Christ. Many times over during my Christian life since I began to learn this truth, I have been prevented from making decisions that would have taken me away from the best that God had for me. Sometimes it has been the timing of a decision. At other times it has been the decision or proposed direction itself.

As a church leader I always encourage people to launch out into new areas in God, and take some risks with the sure knowledge that our heavenly Father is there as the 'everlasting arms' around and under us. I also always assure them that I am there to stand with them both in their successes and failures.

One of the most important keys in these situations is to have the humility and wisdom to admit it when we have made a mistake. We did not hear God after all, or perhaps incompletely. Maybe we were presumptuous or too impetuous. To be able to say both to God, yourself and if necessary fellow Christians, that 'I got it wrong' or 'I made a mistake' is sadly a rare attribute. I may try to point the blame at someone else. People sometimes will even try to level the blame at God, who they feel has let them down. It takes little thought to see the nonsense of this, and more seriously is extremely dishonouring to Him. Instead of trying to defend the indefensible, let us be humble enough to taken on board our own mistakes, learn from them, and go on, asking the Holy Spirit's assistance to sharpen our hearing, and guide us more accurately into truth. In my experience people in the family of God easily forgive and love us when we are honest and vulnerable, and will pick us up and encourage us to have another go with our now freshly adjusted insights! Let us not devalue true faith because of pride.

I trust it is clear that I am in no way playing down or marginalising hope, especially Christian and godly hope. The state of hopelessness is, well, hopeless! It is to be avoided at all costs. As we are born again of the Spirit, it is one of those eternal qualities we receive, and which Paul mentions in 1 Cor. 13:13, along with faith and love. There are many scriptures concerning hope, and having a fixed hope. Paul speaks of a hope that does not disappoint. (Romans 5:5). David in Psalm 42, when he is in exile and under huge pressure, is telling his own soul to hope in God.

In seeking to understand faith, let us not confuse it with hope. Many times what I have been hoping for in God, turns to faith as He assures me by speaking His word into my spirit that my hope will be realised. At that point I no longer have just hope, because I now have His word as substance, and my hope turns to faith. I then know without a shadow of doubt that I shall receive what He has promised. At that point I am able to declare that promise to others even before I have the earthly manifestation of it. You may recall my earlier illustration of aunt's inheritance.

Some years ago, I had found a particular wood stain that was manufactured in the USA and for the purpose for which I was using it, surpassed any equivalent UK product. It took me several months to complete the work in my home, and I had pursued the design and materials with the knowledge that this product was vital to give the final decorative finish to the work. When I came to purchase further supplies of this stain, I found to my dismay that it was no longer being imported from the USA by the chain store from which I had first obtained it. A thorough scouring of all possible suppliers in the UK yielded nothing. I found out the name of the original importer, but they did not have any of the type or colour among their small remaining stock that fitted my requirements. I made attempts through a friend who had family in the USA, to see if they would ship some to me, but this proved impossible as it was classed as inflammable, and there seemed no way of getting it to England either by air or by sea. It was too heavy for carrier pigeon!

I found the issue most frustrating, as the work I had done relied on this particular product, and I could find no suitable alternative whatsoever. I was sharing the whole matter with the Lord on one occasion, asking Him for some wisdom as to what was best to do in the circumstances. I was telling Him of my disappointment, when as clearly as if He was actually talking to me in an audible voice, I heard Him say to me, 'I will get hold of it for you'. I did not need to ask Him to repeat what I had just heard, because I knew it was the Lord speaking. My disappointment turned to joy and faith. I told my wife, my family, and my friends, that I had obtained my stain. Most folks were naturally unimpressed as they understandably could not properly identify with my need, nor understand my excitement. Not only was I about to get my stain, but I also was learning once more that my Father was concerned for the simple everyday things that affected my life. However, a few closer friends who had become aware of my predicament were asking how I had managed to obtain it. 'Oh, I have not got it in my hand yet' I said, 'but I have got it in my faith, because God has promised me ***He*** will obtain it for me'. Some looked quizzically at me – wondering if I was going off my trolley more than usual, but others who knew something deeper of the walk of faith gave me a knowing smile. This saga went on for several weeks, with me getting more certain about the stain I had received, but did not have in my hand, and some of my friends getting more mystified, and beginning rather to mock me in my apparent stupidity. I just quietly went on assuring them that I would have the last laugh.

One lunchtime I arrived back from my morning surgery, and there on the doorstop was a large box. There was no address on it, no postage stamps or other labels indicating any commercial carrier. There was no delivery note, invoice or letter inside, just the two large cans of the stain of exactly the type and colour that I required. I have no idea to this day how it got there, or who brought it, and it cost me absolutely nothing! I still possess a small can of that stain which was left over, as a personal reminder of Father's concern for one of His sons, over a matter which is hardly going to shake the heavens and the earth! It was another step in the Lord's school of faith for me, another lesson in the workings of God.

## CHAPTER 9

# FAITH ON THE INCREASE

~ Jesus said His followers would do greater things than He did. Why don't we then? ~

~ I have received the full amount of faith that I will ever require to fulfil all that God has planned for me to achieve ~

~ Exercise and use of my 'faith muscles' releases my God-given potential. Failure to do so leaves me floppy and ineffective! ~

As my adventure into unknown territory progressed, I found the challenges to my faith increased. It often seemed that while I was having to look constantly to the Lord for His wisdom and help, there would be added incidents that demanded further steps of reliance on Him for provision. One that I remember particularly well concerned my wife Jeanne and our second child Timothy. One morning during my second year at medical school, Jeanne realised that she was short of about £1 to pay the milk bill.(About £25 or $40 at today's prices). At that time it was customary here in the UK to have milk delivered to your door daily. Usually on a Friday the delivery driver would knock on the door and expect to be paid for the milk delivered during the previous week. You were expected to have the money to pay if you required continued delivery of milk for the following week. This particular morning, I had gone to university, and Jeanne had cleared away all the breakfast things, after having taken our older girl to school. On her return she realised that she was short of this money, and as was our habit at these times, she decided to pray and ask the Lord to meet the need. There was no other immediate available source. She sat Timothy on the kitchen work surface, and shared with him what the need was, and that she was going to ask our heavenly Father to supply that need. She began to pray out loud with this request, and she had hardly got into the prayer when Timothy, who rarely shut his eyes during prayer, suddenly exclaimed, 'Look mommy, the money!' There on the end of the kitchen work surface was the one pound. At this point I have to make it clear that the work surface was dark red, completely clear of any clutter, a mark of Jeanne's persistent tidiness, and the one pound was in the form of a bank note, which in those days was about the size of our current ten pound note, and about fifty percent larger than a dollar bill. One could hardly have overlooked its presence beforehand, as it stood out clearly on that dark coloured surface! How did it get there? We had not the slightest idea, nor did it matter, but here was an immediate answer to our need, which our four year old child was able to witness. This was his first lesson in faith, and a further step along the path in our seeing the faithfulness of God towards us.

In my early years as a believer I had picked up the idea that faith came in packets, and that with time and prayer one could accumulate more of these packets. In fairness nobody ever taught me that, but I thought that in this way faith would somehow increase in us as individuals. However, I had to learn as God took me through the new challenges that my everyday life was now presenting, that this was not how it worked at all. Sometimes people will ask me 'how can I get more faith?' Other times when praying for people in a prayer line, some will ask me to pray for them that they can have more faith. I now intend to address this subject.

On the surface it would appear to be quite 'spiritual' to request the Lord to impart to us more faith. After all, if that is what pleases Him, we had better obtain all we can! If that 'which is not of faith is sin' then surely it is most important that we obtain much more. To bolster this argument the disciples themselves asked Jesus for more faith - so it must be right. Well, before we jump to that conclusion, let us examine that passage in Luke 17.

> *'Be on your guard! If your brother sins, rebuke him; and if he repents, forgive him. And if he sins against you seven times a day, and returns to you seven times, saying, 'I repent,' forgive him. And the apostles said to the Lord,* ***'Increase our faith!'*** *And the Lord said, 'If you had faith like a mustard seed, you would say to this mulberry tree, 'Be uprooted and*

*be planted in the sea'; and it would obey you.* Luke 17:3. (Author's emphasis)

Notice that the disciple's request for more faith comes out of Jesus' statement about the need to give repeated forgiveness to someone who continually sins against you. This is a scenario where I like to imagine my listening in to the conversation. As Jesus delivered this answer to Peter's question, I may have observed an incredulous look on the disciples' faces. After all Peter no doubt thinks that he has been extra generous in his suggestion of offering forgiveness up to seven times. Yet Jesus appears to be expecting an almost limitless response of forgiveness instead. Perhaps the disciples were standing there for a while trying to absorb another hard saying from the lips of their Master. Maybe one of them was thinking 'I cannot even imagine how I could follow that directive. That borders on the impossible. After all we are only human!' Now of course all that is speculation, but something must have been going on in their minds along those lines to elicit their response, because we do know that one of them spoke out with the words 'Lord increase our faith!' Did the disciples' request for 'more faith' result from their perception that such extraordinary forgiveness was hard to even imagine, let alone to give? At least their initial conclusion appears to be that they lacked the ability to obey the Lord's injunction without an extra 'dose' of faith.

Now Jesus' reply is most interesting. Notice He does not say to the disciples: 'Well done, that is a very worthy request. Let me lay hands on you for an impartation of more faith.' No, what He shows them is that if they had just the tiniest speck of faith that could be compared with one of the smallest objects that you could identify with your eyes, you could uproot a tree from the ground and tell it to get planted in the sea. Now do you really need more faith? What bigger task do you have to perform right now? I suggest that their request in effect received a mild rebuke, but the incident was a further revelation to them of the operation of faith.

Let us look further into this and at what Paul has to say on the matter:

> *'For through the grace given to me I say to every man among you not to think more highly of himself than he ought to think; but to think so as to have sound judgment* ***as God has allotted to each a measure of faith.'*** Romans 12:3. (Author's emphasis)

The word in the original Greek text translated 'measure' is '***metron'.*** When that word was used in Paul's time it literally meant 'a portion measured off – a determined extent'. Our English words speedo***meter*** and, of course ***meter,*** are derived from that same Greek word, and carry similar meanings. Your electricity meter measures the amount of electrical energy that you have consumed. It is the set amount for which you will be charged. A meter is a predetermined measure of length. So what is this verse telling us? ***'God has allotted to each a measure ( a portion measured off - a determined extent) of faith.'***

That would tell me that I have been freely given as a gift from God, the amount of faith that I will ever require to fulfil all that God in His wisdom has planned for me to achieve in my whole life, assuming that it is lived entirely within the boundaries of His will and purposes for me. I would suggest that it is the same for you. I would even go as far as to suggest that this was the same for Jesus when He was on earth. 'Wow', you say, 'where on earth do you get that from?' We are told quite clearly that Jesus only ever did those things His Father was doing, and He only ever said the things His Father was saying. So if He never went outside His Father's will and purposes, and He received the Holy Spirit's anointing of fullness and power at the commencement of His ministry, why would he need extra 'boosts' of faith from time to time?

This wrong conception about faith being thought of as coming in little 'packages' that get used up, rather like a battery that gets run down and can only produce a certain voltage, really leads us astray. The idea gets formed that either we need more 'packages', recharge the battery, or get a higher voltage one! This I am sure was the sort of idea the disciples had when they asked Jesus to increase their faith. 'We need some more volts to achieve what you are demanding of us!'

What did Jesus mean when on several occasions He upbraided His disciples for their ***lack*** of faith? What did He mean when the Roman centurion came to Him on behalf of his sick servant and was commended for his ***great*** faith? Would this not suggest that the disciples were on a low voltage battery, and the centurion had somehow got a high voltage version? If this were the case then the disciples had better get a new battery!

Let me illustrate what I believe to be the answer in this manner. We will assume we have a pair of identical twin brothers growing up together. We will call them David and Simon. By definition they both have identical genetic constitutions, and there will be pronounced mutual resemblance. For the purpose of our illustration we will also assume that they are identical in their makeup. As they grow up, David develops a very keen interest in fitness, and all things to do with sport. He is one of those strange guys who loves physical education at school! He keenly pursues swimming, rugby, athletics, and mountaineering. He is always in the gymnasium and even gets into weight lifting. He is very particular about the quality and content of what he eats. In fact he is hardly ever at home except for his regular sleeping pattern. His whole life revolves around physical activity.

Simon, on the other hand for no apparent reason, develops an absolute aversion to anything that requires any physical effort at all. He is physically lazy, and from a child will be found slumped in front of the television set. His sporting activities are solely confined to raising his fisted hand and punching the air every time the football team he supports scores. This is always viewed on the television of course, as the effort to get to the football ground one mile away is completely off limits for him. The only time he will ever be persuaded to bestir himself will be for a trip to the local fryer for a portion of battered sausage, chips and a coke. Simon is, not surprisingly, grossly overweight.

Their mother is involved in raising funds for various worthy charities, and somehow persuades both her boys to get involved in a sponsored weight lifting competition. David gets to 120 kg. lifted above his head. Simon just about manages 20kg. briefly and collapses! How strange, these young men are identical twins. Why the profound difference, when they were both given the same 'equipment' at birth? The answer is plainly obvious to us all. David, through rigorous use and training has developed his muscular potential to the full. Simon has not, and it certainly shows. We know that it is no use Simon asking God for some more muscle power to be equal to his brother. We suspect that the divine command would be 'Get off your backside, eat a good diet and get down to the gym for some hard work!' We also know, providing this is what Simon does, and keeps working at it, in the process of time he also will be able to lift the 120kg. In that of course we assume that he has not done some irreparable damage to himself from his previous lifestyle.

The moral and message of this scenario is that we do not require 'more faith'. What we are required to do is to ***use*** the faith we have already been given by God! In the regular use of our apportioned measure of faith our 'faith muscles' will develop progressively. Bearing in mind that a 'mustard seed' measure will transplant trees and shift whole mountains, most of us have a long way to go before we need to go bleating to God that we have reached our full potential, and could He do something about it. In fact Jesus made it clear that the potential of His followers would be greater than His had been!

*'Truly, truly, I say to you, he who believes in Me, the works that I do shall he do also; and* ***greater works than these shall he do;*** *because I go to the Father. And whatever you ask in My name, that will I do, that the Father may be glorified in the Son. If you ask Me anything in My name, I will do it.'* John 14:12-14. (Author's emphasis)

I am aware of the theological arguments that range over this verse. Did Jesus really mean that His followers, after He had returned to the Father, and under the Acts 2 outpouring of the Holy Spirit, would perform greater miracles than He did? Did He mean greater in quantity or in quality and power? Or did He really mean that now there would be hundreds, then thousands of followers, all anointed with the same Holy Spirit with which He was anointed, and therefore the quantity would be greatly magnified. The problem is that while the discussions and convictions range back and forth, I have to ask if there is anybody taking this statement of Jesus, and in faith in His word, going out there and actually starting to perform some works! Just ***some*** works at least to explore the possibility! Well, what about ***one*** work.

Sadly the church over the years has erected very effective theological smoke screens to excuse our powerlessness and ineffectiveness. When we have failed to hear and obey the very clear injunctions of the word of God, by taking the 'faith muscle' that we have, and putting it to work, we then have to come up with a good reason why the scripture is apparently not working. Rather than say 'I am not seeing anything in the way of miraculous works from my ministry. Lord where are the 'greater works' that You promised, and where am I going wrong. Please reveal it to me', we eventually construct a theological reason for our failure and absence of power. 'Well of course the scripture does not actually mean that'. We then end up believing the reason for our unbelief, not realising that we are in unbelief, and believing that the Lord is pleased with our position! I think the term for that is deception - gross deception!

Many of us have heard stories of people who have been born again, who read their bibles, and who just go off and do what it says. Without any element of surprise they begin to pray for sick people and they get healed time and time again. There are verified accounts of such folks seeing the dead come to life after laying hands on them. They have not even read a manual on faith. If you asked them to define faith, they would probably look at you as if you were mad. 'Faith – what is that?' Eventually they join a church, and are taught that those things do not happen today! 'It is not quite that easy, brother,' they are told. Our green new convert is left thinking 'Well it was. I just read my bible and literally did what it said!' Wise 'spiritual' sages, shake their heads patronisingly and say 'That young believer has got a lot to learn'. Then God please deliver him from such 'wise spiritual sages' because they will kill this guy's effectiveness for kingdom advance.

Jesus said: 'Greater works than these shall he (singular) do, because I go to the Father.' Please notice that it does not read 'Greater works shall you [plural] do...' Is it not time for the people of God to step up to their high calling in Christ as Spirit-indwelt sons of God, and begin to flex their 'faith muscles' by starting to act on what He has said and promised? If a mustard seed of faith can move a mountain, we certainly do not need any more until we are required to move two mountains, and by then perhaps our 'muscles' will have developed to such an extent even that will not be a problem!

# CHAPTER 10

# THE HEARING OF FAITH

~ By walking close to the Shepherd, you will hear what He says. Wandering around at the back of the flock, you won't hear much! ~

~ God's desire to speak to us, is far greater than our preparedness to listen. We need a major paradigm shift in our minds to embrace the implications ~

It should be clear to my readers by now that the vital key to faith is being able to listen and hear the voice of God. If faith comes by hearing God's voice then it must be important to be able to recognize and appropriate what God is saying to us. While this is not a book about hearing God's voice – there are many current excellent books available that deal with this subject – I want to include a chapter on this issue as it is so closely related and essential if we are to develop a life of faith.

Over the years, many Christians have asked me how do I know when I have heard God speak to me. They say, 'If faith actually comes by hearing the word that God is speaking, how do you know when it is His voice, your own inner voice, or even the devil's voice?' It is an excellent question, and one for which we all have to find the answer. I am fully aware that the people of God hear His voice in a whole variety of ways, so what I am about to share with a few examples is by no means exhaustive. Nevertheless these are some of the ways that I have experienced hearing the voice of God, and I trust that from them you will be helped to be able to hear Him more clearly for yourself.

I recall an occasion in the second year of my medical course when I faced my first viva voce examination in anatomy. This was where you come face to face with one of the lecturers in the subject and are asked questions, and expected to discuss various anatomical features of parts of the body that you had dissected over several previous weeks. As this was the first of a new experience, I was very apprehensive about the encounter, and after the formalities of introducing myself to my examiner, I found my mind went completely blank. There was not one single anatomical fact anywhere in my brain. Not one anywhere at all – I was looking in every cupboard! 'Ask me how a helicopter can fly backwards, and I will tell you in detail, sir, but please, this is not the day for anatomy!' He perhaps saw the misery on my face, and I think decided to let me in gently. He handed me a bone from the upper arm, whose name I promptly forgot in my panic. I can hear his question now as clearly as when he uttered it well over thirty-five years ago. 'Could you tell me what this is?' he asked gently. A question that probably anyone straight off the street outside might have had a good crack at answering. With great clarity and a sudden rush of insight I replied, 'A bone, sir!' 'Very good, Wood' he replied somewhat laconically. 'Would you like to hazard a guess at the name of it?' Everything in me wanted to say 'No sir, I would not. Please can I leave now? – sir!' Suddenly I remembered that I had a heavenly Father who had not only directed and encouraged me into this path in the first place, but who had promised to be with me, and hold my hand and help me at all times. I needed Him right now! 'Oh Lord, please!' Immediately my panic ceased and my brain cleared. 'A humerus', I announced with a sudden rush of anatomical insight. 'Would you like to suggest whether it is right one or a left one?' 'A right one', I said with growing confidence, pointing out a feature on the bone that determined this. I was now on a roll, and the questions continued and the answers came. The last question was always the hardest, and was designed to sort out the A+ grading from the A's. 'Can you describe sub-clavian stealing?' I had never ever heard of it, and did not even know whether the 'stealing' was spelt steeling or stealing! I knew 'sub-clavian' referred to an artery, vein or nerve, situated beneath the collar-bone, but that did not seem helpful. Suddenly into my mind came the clear picture of the blood vessels in that region that I had dissected and studied in the recent past few weeks. To my amazement I heard myself giving quite a complex answer that I could never have thought up myself. This time it was my examiner who ended up clearly looking impressed! What at first began to look like a disaster, became a triumph as I was able to settle my fears and anxiety and relax into hearing the wisdom of God for that occasion.

I am sure most of you will have met Christians who claim to hear the voice of God about some issue in their lives which takes them off at a tangent, only to hear that God has spoken again, and they are off in the opposite direction within days or weeks. I get rather dizzy with such people. It is rather like watching a tennis match from the net! These dear people are often following their own desires and intents rather than truly discovering the voice of God and His will for their lives. If I allowed myself to be cynical, and did not know better, I could end up beginning to get the impression that even God could not make up His mind what they should do, which clearly is absolute nonsense.

I mentioned earlier, that I grew up with the conviction that God never said anything, except perhaps to those who were very old and very spiritual. Any books that I picked up on the subject seemed very old, very thick and very boring, and rarely brought forth any meaningful revelation on the subject that I could comprehend! Then one day I was reading John's gospel, and the passage in chapter ten where Jesus is talking about shepherds and sheep. I was reading this passage probably for at least the hundredth time, and it was so familiar I hardly needed to read the actual words. Yet on this occasion a statement by Jesus jumped out of the page and suddenly brought light and a fresh understanding which turned all that upside down for me.

> *'My sheep hear My voice, and I know them, and they follow Me'* John 10:27.

That sounds pretty straightforward, doesn't it? ***'My sheep hear My voice.'*** Out went all my old dry dusty books. Out went all my preconceptions about the impossibility of ever hearing God speak. Out went my idea that only the old and learned stood a chance.

I have no firsthand experience as a sheep farmer, but I see them regularly in the fields adjacent to my home which is in a very rural setting. I do know that they often act pretty stupidly and are not exactly the most intelligent of the animal world. On my walks across these fields I have on more than one occasion given one or other of them my counsel and advice when they have become stuck behind a fence that they should not have gone through in the first place. It was always to no avail. Either they did not understand English or were too proud to admit their mistake. Perhaps they were just plain stupid. I did not know whether to be affronted or pleased to be called a sheep! However, one thing I did realise from this verse was that if a sheep can learn to hear the shepherd's voice, then it must be pretty easy as one of ***His*** sheep, for me to hear the voice of the Lord. It also became clear that to the shepherd, each sheep was individually known, and that His voice was such that the sheep wanted to follow it.

Often when I receive these rather intrusive telephone sales calls asking for me personally, I say 'Do I know you?' But when my wife Jeanne telephones, I do not say 'Who are you?' and she does not reply 'Is that Stephen?' Of course not, as we have known each other intimately for over forty years. You could parade thousands of voices past my ear, but I guarantee I could pick out hers immediately. In the same way we soon are able to pick out the Lord's voice from all the other 'noise' and voices that are going on around us. It comes from intimacy with Him. From spending time with Him. From 'seeking His face' as the scriptures often describe it.

If you are walking close to the Shepherd, you will hear what He has to say. If you wander off and spend most of your time at the 'back of the flock' then it is highly likely you will miss most of what He has to say, and you will end up convinced that it is difficult to hear the voice of the Lord. Living by faith will probably prove very difficult. The problem will not be His, but yours. For people who say to me that they never hear God speak to them, I ask them if they ever spend time getting to know Him, and ***listening***. Many Christians spend the whole of their prayer time talking to God, and outlining all their needs. I have learnt sometimes to put myself close to Him, say nothing, ask nothing, and just listen.

I recall happy times when as a teenager my father and I would be working on some project, and we would just chat about a whole variety of things as we worked together. Most of it would not be of any great importance. In fact, my father who always seemed to remember the humorous side of his life would often recount these tales, and we would laugh and joke together. While I would sometimes ask my father for certain things, or to help and advise me over some matter, this was a relatively small part of my relationship with him.

As I was learning to hear my heavenly Father's voice, I began to realise that in my communication with Him I talked incessantly only about the things that concerned me, punctuated with requests for Him to sort out issues. My relationship with Him consisted of 'Please will you do this, please will you sort that, please will you give me this, oh and by the way I need that that and that, and why has this happened? I would never have dreamt of talking to my earthly father in that way, and if I had, assuming he would have let me, anybody listening in to the conversation certainly would come to the conclusion that we had a very poor one-sided relationship. It is what I call an 'ATM relationship' – I pop my card in, and expect my request to pop out! I have no fellowship at all with the machinery on the other side of the wall!

I have developed a love for regular walking in the countryside, and where I live in England, there are old country lanes, and farm tracks, and rights of way across fields, where one can wander freely and enjoy the hills and valleys and the general scenery. As I walk I love to fellowship with the Lord as I ask Him to come with me. Sometimes I just listen to anything He might wish to share with me. Sometimes I chat with Him about the countryside, admiring with Him its beauty, thanking Him for His wonderful creation, and for my human senses that can enjoy it all. On one occasion when ploughing up a very steep incline, I asked Him rather breathlessly if He was coping alright! I had the distinct sense in my spirit of Him saying 'It rather looks as if it is ***you*** that is struggling!' If that sort of thing surprises or even shocks you, then why? Surely you would chat like that when out with an intimate friend? If Jesus is your best friend, why would you not learn to converse like that? Many times on these occasions He has directed my attention to some object or natural occurrence as we have been walking, and spoken prophetically and often very powerfully to me from it.

Sometimes I am overwhelmed by His love and provision for me. In it all I end up wanting to hear His will for my life and pursue it. God's voice becomes clearer the more I spend time pursuing Him. Why make it more complicated than that? We so easily buy into Satan's lies, which sadly can often become enshrined in 'Christian' dogma, but which are entirely untrue and unbiblical. I cannot assess how many times in my early Christian upbringing I was either told, or it was inferred that it was very difficult to hear the voice of God. Yet the scriptures are full of people who heard God clearly speak to them and direct them. It is important to observe however, that where God spoke and the recipient or recipients ignored and disobeyed His voice, that their ears became dull of hearing, and the Lord stopped speaking. But there is no biblical account of which I am aware that suggests God has a reluctance in any way to communicate with anyone who has a genuine desire to listen. If that were true you certainly would never have got born again.

The Lord speaking through the prophet Jeremiah to the nation of Israel about their promised restoration from Babylonian captivity makes this promise:

> *'Then you will call upon Me and come and pray to Me,* ***and I will listen to you.*** *'And you will seek Me and find Me,* ***when you search for Me*** *with all your heart.* ***'And I will be found by you,'*** *declares the LORD.* Jer. 29:12-14. (Author's emphasis)

We need to know that God is more desiring to speak to us, than we are ready to listen, most of the time. There is need in many of us for a major paradigm shift in our minds in order to embrace, believe and act on this.

I find it is most interesting that it was the disciple John who said 'My sheep hear My voice'. The picture that the gospels give us of this man was clearly one of intimacy with the Lord. He appears singled out from the other disciples as the 'disciple who Jesus loved', an appellation he appears to have used for himself, but not, I would presume without reason. Neither must we draw the conclusion from this that Jesus did not love any of the others. That was clearly not true. We also read the phrase that during meals John was found 'leaning on Jesus' breast'. Now to our western minds that is a strange concept, especially as we normally have our meals sitting in a chair and often at a table. But in the homes that Jesus frequented it was normal to recline at floor level on one's side when partaking of a meal. I image the picture of John reclining right in front of Jesus, in such a way that his head at times was close to Jesus' chest. Now it does not take much imagination to expect that John would hear things that Jesus would say, that others in the room might miss. It might even have been that Jesus would quietly say things to John that were not for general hearing. In fact in reading the gospel and epistles of John, he clearly expresses deep heart issues about God and His love, that other writers do not. So it was John, the disciple of intimacy, that has told us that as His sheep we have the capacity to hear Him speaking to us. John was certainly one sheep that did – very clearly.

While I know there are other considerations and other ways that God speaks to us, at least let us start to pursue the simple. When my children were young, as their father, I did not try to speak to them in Latin or German when their whole environment had been English. I did not say, 'Now children I am going to speak in riddles and in code, and your job is to sort it out. If you do not, you will fail understand what I am saying, and this might well get you into trouble' You would rightly think, what sort of a crazy dad is he? Yet so many Christians seem to believe that their heavenly Father operates on something like this basis.

My total confidence rests on those simple words of Jesus. If you are one of His flock, and have an open ear and a desire to hear the good shepherd, then you ***will*** hear His voice. Jesus did not say 'My sheep might hear My voice', or 'My sheep may occasionally hear My voice', or 'My very old, wise and excellently behaved sheep will hear My voice'!

Sometimes, you will need to put some specific time aside to just quieten your spirit. So often our days are filled with external noise that constantly clamours for our attention, and internally our soul may be full of questions, fears and unhelpful emotions. We have to learn to relax in the comfort and security of His sheepfold, in the confidence of His love and acceptance, and thus make ourselves ready to hear His voice.

I referred in chapter 6 to an occasion when I needed desperately to hear the voice of God in respect of His help concerning a particular examination that I was facing. On another occasion during my third year as a medical student, I had had a series of three quite major examinations in different subjects that had been set one after the other with little space for any serious revision time. I came to the final one of the series, an examination in biochemistry, with far too little time for detailed revision. As often seemed to happen, at that same time I was having to deal with some pressing pastoral problems in the church in which I was a leader. It was one of those situations where you have a suspicion that the Lord has gently set you up in order for you to learn a fresh lesson! Here again I needed some help, and some direction into the limited revision time that I had left to me. With a growing trust in the Lord's enabling in these circumstances, and a confidence that He had promised to be a strength and help to me, I knew that I needed to put time aside to converse with Him about this examination!

I can picture the very place and the occasion clearly. I sat down with a pen and a blank sheet of paper, and just began to relax and lay any anxiety and pressure that the situation was generating aside. 'Father, You are aware I need wisdom right now, to devote the time I have available to study relevant subjects. I open my inner ears to receive Your voice and the impartation of that wisdom to me.' As I lay back in my chair, biochemical subjects and topics began to come into my mind. I quickly began to write them down one after the other until I had nine specific areas outlined. To say I was encouraged was an understatement, and over the remaining time that I had available, I revised and studied these nine topics.

When I was faced with the examination paper, out of the eight questions on the paper, seven of them were directly related to the topics I had studied and done revision on, and in a further examination some weeks later I was examined on one of the other two remaining areas. I never discovered why I had spent time on the last remaining subject. Probably the Lord felt I needed to know about it anyway, but I was quite satisfied that eight out of nine was a good score! 'My sheep hear My voice and they follow Me'.

Some may still ask how you can know it is not your own inner voice driven by what you may want to hear, or even the voice of the enemy? Is not there a danger of being deceived? It would be foolish to deny any absence of danger, and some helpful soul has suggested that faith is spelt r-i-s-k! However, I have always had full confidence that when I actively place my trust and the direction of my life into the hands of my heavenly Father, I can rely on His faithfulness and power to keep me from deception, and know the promise of the Holy Spirit to guide me into all truth. Hearing God is equally a walk of faith in ***His*** ability, as well as mine. His power to guide me is infinitely greater than is Satan's ability to deceive me. I am unable to accept that when I come in simple trust to hear from my heavenly Father, He will allow the enemy to push in front with some deceptive word to throw me off track. Luke 11:10-13 is a great assurance on this issue. I also believe that when I have a heart to hear and do the will of God, the Holy Spirit makes it clear if I am pursuing an entirely selfish agenda.

# CHAPTER 11

# THE DYNAMIC OF FAITH

~ Faith is not passive. It is an ***active*** walking out on what God is saying ~

~ Old covenant men and women were reckoned by God as righteous through their faith! ~

~ God can make ways where there are no ways, and bring means where there are none, to the man and woman of faith! ~

Faith, given to us by the Holy Spirit, releases all the potential of heaven into earthly situations. It creates the means for God's will to be done on earth as it is always being done in heaven. It makes what is naturally impossible - possible. As we continue to develop our understanding of faith, we see that it is essentially an ***active*** relying on the living Word of God, which has the power to produce God's promised result. Faith is never ***passive***! Faith ***activates*** the spirit realm.

We may trust in God because of His impeccable track record, and while this is good and necessary, it can be purely passive. We can believe in God, and so we should, but this again can be passive. The devil and his demons undoubtedly have this kind of belief in God! We can trust and believe in the safety and reliability of our car, but you could never have a true active biblical faith in it to produce something supernatural. In fact a wheel may fall off, rendering even your basic confidence in it unfounded!

In Genesis15:6 we read that ***'Abraham believed God'*** not in a passive way, but in an active, vibrant, situation-changing way. Faith is, as it were, the key that unlocks a door, enabling the dynamic of the power of God into situations. It is our response on earth to the will of God in heaven. I am in no way suggesting that God could not break into any situation that He so desired. He is sovereign over everything His hand has created. However, He has chosen through the exercise of our faith to accomplish His will and purposes here.

The apostle Paul in Romans 4 outlines the ***power*** of faith in the life of Abraham to effect the impossible. He was a man with a record of regular obedience to God, and a heart to follow God's ways. We see that although far from perfect, he had an impressive track record. He had a lot to boast about, if he was trying to win God's favour and approval. But it was not that which would impress God in the slightest. He was not 'justified by works'!

> *'What then shall we say that Abraham, our forefather according to the flesh, has found? For if Abraham was justified by works, he has something to boast about; but not before God. For what does the Scripture say? 'And Abraham believed God, and it was reckoned to him as righteousness' Now to the one who works, his wage is not reckoned as a favour, but as what is due. But to the one who does not work, but believes in Him who justifies the ungodly, his faith is reckoned as righteousness.'* Romans 4:1-5.

It is truly remarkable that Abraham's faith was '***reckoned to him as righteousness***.' God, being just, would not overlook Abraham's sinful nature (inherited from Adam), even though it is most likely that he had tried to live a life pleasing to God from the time he responded to God's call. The sentence of death for sin was in force, but, it was Abraham's ***active faith*** through putting his full unshakable and unswerving confidence in the living word of God to him, that made him righteous before God. It is all the more remarkable to us that Abraham was reckoned righteous, since Jesus had not yet died to take away the sin that separated man from God. Yet Abraham was made righteous - by his faith! Faith had the power to invade Abraham's life with the future age of grace. We have to bear in mind that prior to the saving work of Christ on the cross, there was no person that could die for the sins of another. The outlook for humankind was bleak following Adam and Eve's transgression - it was called death! It started with immediate spiritual death, followed by eventual physical death.

Even when God's law was revealed to Moses and so to the nation of Israel, it soon became evident even before it was properly inaugurated, that the human race was no nearer coming out of the pit that it had dug for itself. There was certainly no human act or words that would bridge the infinite gap between a holy God and a sinful man or woman. The immeasurable quantity of animal blood that was shed in sacrifices to temporarily atone for sin, could never eradicate the eventual judgment of a holy God on a single one of them, or deal with the real root issues of the heart. All it could do was temporarily avert it. It would appear that Abraham's faith and obedience to God's word, carried him over into the present age of God's grace, when Christ would pay the full sentence for his sins, and he would enter the kingdom on the same basis that we have. This would be true for all the other men and women of faith who lived prior to the cross of Christ – they were put 'on hold', waiting for the revealing of God's wonderful plan of salvation. Many of these are listed along with Abraham in Hebrews chapter 11.

Earlier in the same epistle we learn more about the power in the word:

> *'For the word of God is living and active and sharper than any two-edged sword, and piercing as far as the division of soul and spirit, of both joints and marrow, and able to judge the thoughts and intentions of the heart.'* Hebrews 4:12.

The word of God has the power to pierce and unearth issues – between that which is of the spirit and that which is of the soul. How many times do believers pursue something that they feel is God's will for their lives, yet underlying it is a soulish desire or pursuit?

I recall an occasion soon after we were married. I had the offer of a job in an area of the country where I had always wanted to live. I quickly found a lovely house that we could afford, in a quiet rural setting. There was a scenic route to work in an attractive spa town, and there was a church in that town very similar to our own that we were attending at that time. The very day we moved in we connected with other Christians who lived no more than a mile away. Clearly God was on our case. It fitted everything I desired. Surely this must be the will of God. Only it was not! It proved to be a complete disaster, and within a year we were back in the same town, the same church and the same job! You see, I had failed to open my life to that powerful word of God that could divide between what ***I*** wanted and what ***He*** wanted. There has to come the conviction within us, that the word of God has the power to accomplish anything that God chooses to utter.

> *'For as the rain and the snow come down from heaven, and do not return there without watering the earth, and making it bear and sprout, and furnishing seed to the sower and bread to the eater; So shall My word be which goes forth from My mouth; It shall not return to Me empty,* ***without accomplishing what I desire,*** *and without succeeding in the matter for which I sent it'.* Isaiah 55.10-11. (Author's emphasis)

We hear what God says, place our entire trust in Him, and move out in obedience to it, then the creative power of that word comes into effect in our lives. I almost picture it as if we hear His word and then 'jump on the back' of it, and we are carried through to God's certain goal in that thing.

I remember well the day that I had finished my final year as a medical student. The day of reckoning had arrived when the results would be posted up in the medical school. Had we jumped the interminable hurdles that our examiners had set for us to clear? (So much for the 'continual assessment' idea that had triggered this journey in the first place – I found out when it was too late the truth would be better expressed as 'continual examination'!) Had we been deemed fit to take the very lives of the public into our hands? Some students dared not go and look, but sent colleagues to bear the news to them. As I quickly scanned to the bottom of the alphabetical list - the place where my surname always resided - there was my name! I had successfully graduated after six years of a journey with God that in human terms was impossible and still seemed incredible.

I remember that moment so clearly. Yes, there was the elation of success after all the years of hard work in study and application. It would be a strange student who did not feel some pleasure in achievement. However, it was also a deeply emotional moment that I shared with the Lord in front of that examination results board in the entrance foyer of Birmingham Medical School that day. It was the emotion that resulted from Father and me doing something together for six years which had changed my relationship with Him forever. It had been my first real walk of faith in the invisible God, who was my Father. He had spoken into my life, and for the first time I had actually taken Him at His word and jumped off the precipice into the unknown impossibilities that I knew awaited me. It had been an astounding ride, with victories and apparent defeats; highs and lows; provision in advance, and nail-biting eleventh hour potential disasters. I had 'jumped on the back' of His word, and from learning to put my full confidence in it, He had brought about the impossible.

As I stood there fighting back the tears that were arising in me from the knowledge and realisation of the faithfulness of God, I recall saying to Him, 'Father, well done, You have obtained for Yourself another degree in Medicine and Surgery, because this result does not belong to me.' Then I heard His reply in my spirit, 'Not so son, it is ***ours***, we did it together!' By now I am an emotional wreck, and any onlooker would have concluded I had completely failed the course!

It is so easy as believers, as someone else has put it, to talk the talk of faith, instead of walking the walk of faith. We can talk it, discuss it, read about it, get a sound theology about it, but in the end God's requirement is that we walk it!

After he had journeyed some twenty-four years with God, one day Abraham experienced another significant visitation from the Lord.

> *'Now when Abram was ninety-nine years old, the Lord appeared to Abram and said to him, 'I am God Almighty; Walk before Me, and be blameless.'* Genesis 17:1.

Let us now use our imagination a little and try to re-live the scene. God on this occasion appears to Abraham with this request. I wonder how Abraham felt? He had been privileged to have had such exchanges with God on previous occasions, and his walk with God had progressed over the years. Did Abraham think another test as it had been with Isaac was coming? Of course we do not know, but it is most unlikely that he expected ***this*** call and opportunity. God on declaring again to Abraham his power and might, invites him into perhaps the closest fellowship with Himself imaginable. I understand that a rendering of the Hebrew word translated 'walk before', has within in it the meaning 'walk eye to eye with' or 'face to face with'. Wow, what an invitation! Can you see the power and blessings that God was releasing through His grace to this man, as a result of his faith? Clearly this was a call to a life of holiness - 'be blameless'. Can you imagine having a call from God to walk daily in face to face contact with Him? Well, please stop imagining, because that is ***your*** calling too, and through faith you can! As with Abraham, in the same way the fruit of our walking in increasing fellowship with the Almighty will result in the transformation of our lives. That which the scripture calls 'sanctification', being made holy or 'set apart'.

This scenario always reminds me of that wonderful enjoyment and fellowship with God, that Adam and Eve had before they sinned, and that which David enjoyed, and who also heard God say to him –

'Seek My face', with David's eager heart's response - 'Your face, O Lord, I shall seek' (Psalm 27:8).

It has been said that 'God makes ways where there are no ways!' Regarding God's promise that Abraham would have a son from his first wife Sarah, he fully realised that at one hundred years of age his reproductive abilities were as good as dead. He also looked at his equally elderly wife who had been through the menopause years ago. He had fully assessed what he knew to be the facts and in human terms he was faced with an impossibility. Notwithstanding his thoughts about such outward 'evidence', Abraham 'grew strong in faith' and 'gave glory to God.' Now please read this passage through carefully, and note Abraham's reactions to the 'impossible'.

> *For this reason it is by faith, that it might be in accordance with grace, in order that the promise may be certain* ***to all the descendants,*** *not only to those who are of the Law,* ***but also to those who are of the faith of Abraham, who is the father of us all,*** *(as it is written 'a father of many nations have I made you') in the sight of Him whom he believed, even God, who gives life to the dead* ***and calls into being that which does not exist.*** *In hope against hope he believed, in order that he might become a father of many nations, according to that which had been spoken,* ***'so shall your descendants be. And without becoming weak in faith he contemplated his own body,*** *now as good as dead since he was about a hundred years old, and the deadness of Sarah's womb; yet, with respect to the promise of God,* ***he did not waver in unbelief, but grew strong in faith,*** *giving glory to God, and being* ***fully assured*** *that what He had promised, He was able also to perform.'* Romans 4:16-21. (Author's emphasis)

God 'calls into being that which does not exist'. I think that makes a nuclear explosion look rather like damp match! When we walk by faith in what God has said, 'impossibilities' have to yield to God's kingdom invading this earth. There is the unlimited creative power of God behind the walk of faith.

While we do not always see the earthly manifestation of our faith, as we learn from Hebrews 11:13, our active living faith in Him and His promises coupled with obedience is what matters. Many of those who have gone before us, while in their flesh did not see that earthly manifestation, they 'welcomed them from a distance', seeing clearly into the realm of reality that was yet to come. Faith expands the realm of our daily living beyond the natural and enables us to embrace the reality of the eternal - now.

# Chapter 12

# Faith is for Now

~ Whenever God's will is done on earth, His kingdom is manifest as an invasion into the natural realm ~

~ Might it just be that in this day the people of God would begin to realise their divine and powerful calling, and begin to live by faith? ~

I have found, and continue to find, many believers who only have conviction and 'faith' for the future. They think life here on earth is really a holding operation while we wait for the 'summing up of all things', when our life in Christ will really start. I make it my practice to ask fellow believers how they are when I greet them. I usually get the classic reply 'Fine' except from those who really know me. 'Fine?' I say, 'what does that mean, I was not asking about the weather?' 'Oh, so so.' Right, I say, 'I wasn't asking about your needlework either. I was asking about you!' 'Well, hanging in there I guess.' The mind boggles. Hanging in where, on what and for how long? Now of course we all know what we mean by these polite interchanges – absolutely nothing! We are not giving anything away to anybody – probably not God either, forgetting He knows the full details anyway. What a joy sometimes to meet someone who says, 'I am doing really well, because God loves me, and I am filled with the Spirit, and I am living by faith. However, it is tough right now, and we are having some problems with the children, but thanks for asking – I appreciate your care', or at least some version of that. That tells me that they are living in the reality of life in Christ in the here and now. So many believers appear to be 'hanging on' to life just waiting for the return of the Lord to get us all out of the mess that the human race has made for itself.

I guess I have always had an enquiring mind and as a young developing child I am sure I was sometimes a pain in the neck to my parents. I always wanted to know how things worked, and I was no different in my attitude to the scriptures. I began to notice what to me was a strange phrase in the light of this idea that all was 'on hold' for some undetermined day in the future.

John the Baptist appears on the scene with a rather singular message, which Jesus takes up immediately ***He*** begins His ministry. 'Repent for the kingdom of heaven is a hand'. Now I had learned that repentance was all about changing one's mind and direction, but what was this 'kingdom of heaven' that was supposed to be 'at hand' or 'has come near you', which is perhaps a more helpful translation. Further enquiry from my more 'experienced' elders in the faith suggested that this kingdom of heaven was in the future, and had little relevance for the here and now. How strange. 'At hand' and 'Has come near you' did not sound like more than two thousand years away.

I also knew the prayer that Jesus taught His disciples: 'Your kingdom come, your will be done on earth as it is being done in heaven'. Praying those words seemed to me to be a total waste of time if God had predetermined the occasion when His kingdom would come, which was obviously by now at least two thousand years since Jesus mentioned it! My mentors told me not to worry my head about it as it was definitely all for the future when Jesus returned to earth. Then I read another passage which added to confusion.

> *'Then there was brought to Him a demon-possessed man who was blind and dumb, and He healed him, so that the dumb man spoke and saw. And all the multitudes were amazed, and began to say, 'This man cannot be the Son of David, can he?' But when the Pharisees heard it, they said, 'This man casts out demons only by Beelzebul the ruler of the demons.' And knowing their thoughts He said to them, 'Any kingdom divided against itself is laid waste; and any city or house divided against itself shall not stand. And if Satan casts out Satan, he is divided against himself; how then shall his kingdom stand? And if I by Beelzebul cast out demons, by whom do your sons cast them out? Consequently they shall be your judges.'* Matthew 12:22-27.

Jesus when confronted with demons was aware of His Father's will for that situation. Jesus did not have to shout, jump up and down, or name the demon. Jesus spoke the Word of the Father in which He has absolute faith – remember 'faith comes by hearing the Word of God'. As expected the demon left immediately. Then you get the response of the Pharisees – at the end of which Jesus makes this statement:

> *'.... if I cast out demons by the Spirit of God,* ***then the kingdom of God has come upon you.'*** Matthew 12:22-28. (Author's emphasis)

It seemed to me that Jesus, when confronted with this precious man and setting him free, was clearly saying, the very fact that the demon had been cast out of him, was evidence that the kingdom of God had just invaded his life, there and then. In BC 2 or whatever! It certainly did not seem to be two thousand years away still! There had just been a clear manifestation of the power of the kingdom of heaven. It certainly was to that man – at hand. Jesus knew that He had been assigned a clear task to fulfil as a man on this earth. So often Christians, when asked what that assignment was, would say that He came to die for the sins of the world. Now while that fact is quite true of course, if that were the full purpose of His coming, why would He want to take twelve pretty rough men, and pour over three years of His life into them, teaching them and training them practically in the gospel of the kingdom? Surely all Jesus needed to do was be born, grow up into adulthood to prove to all His sinlessness, then die on the cross. Job done! Ah, you say, He needed some folks who would carry on with the work. What work? There was certainly no need of another crucifixion, and His followers were anything but sinless anyway.

The death and resurrection of Jesus was the guarantee by faith to all humankind of entrance into the kingdom of heaven, but unless we knew there ***was*** a kingdom to enter, and unless we knew how to enter it, and unless we knew about the King of the kingdom, we would be left ignorant. The earthly mission of Jesus, was to 'be about His Father's business', which was to reveal who the Father was, and the power of His Father's kingdom:

> *'Philip said to Him, 'Lord, show us the Father, and it is enough for us.' Jesus said to him, 'Have I been so long with you, and yet you have not come to know Me, Philip? He who has seen Me has seen the Father; how do you say, 'Show us the Father'? Do you not believe that I am in the Father, and the Father is in Me? The words that I say to you I do not speak on My own initiative, but the Father abiding in Me does His works'.* John 14:8-10.

> *'... the words which You gave Me I have given to them; and they received them, and truly understood that I came forth from You, and they believed that You did send Me....... and I have made Your name known to them, and will make it known; that the love with which You loved Me may be in them, and I in them.'* John 17:8&26.

Jesus came to be a living representation and illustration of the Father. A living illustration of the love of God for fallen humankind. A living illustration of the King who had a realm of rule that could impact their lives now, and that they could enter and draw on every day of their earthly lives, by faith in the living word of God.

When I was very young Christian, while I understood that Jesus was born as a man, I had the idea that when needed He switched into some sort of 'God-mode' and performed miracles! This is so far from the truth. Scripture tells us He 'laid aside' many aspects of His deity, when coming to earth, albeit to take them up again on return to His Father. He was born a baby. He learned to walk and talk. He learned obedience. He faced temptation, but did not sin. The scripture says that 'He learned obedience from the things which He suffered'

Hebrews 5:8. He is our perfect example of faith, because He learned to always hear and obey His Father's word. Through that word of faith, the sick were healed, the demonised delivered, the dead raised, the storms stilled, and water turned to wine. Every time He spoke the word of faith into a situation it changed, as He brought the rule and authority of God. The kingdom of heaven invaded the situation immediately, and the will of God was done on earth as it was being done in heaven. It was a powerful invasion of the eternal into the temporal which had to bow to it. Of course demons had to flee. Of course sickness had to go. Of course death was vanquished.

Most Christians would readily accept that there is no cancer in heaven, or any other sickness. There are no demons in heaven. There are no demonic storms in heaven. There would be no problem walking on water in heaven if there were any! 'Your will be done on earth as it is in heaven' seems to me to be a complete waste of time if God is going to bring that about at the end of the age anyway. It is no more than a statement of longing for something better, but no hope of it being released in the present.

We know that Jesus did not confine the bringing of God's kingdom to earth to Himself. He taught the disciples to be involved, again stating the immediacy of this kingdom:

> *'And He was saying to them, The harvest is plentiful, but the labourers are few; therefore beseech the Lord of the harvest to send out labourers into His harvest. Go your ways; behold, I send you out as lambs in the midst of wolves. Carry no purse, no bag, no shoes; and greet no one on the way. And whatever house you enter, first say, 'Peace be to this house.' And if a man of peace is there, your peace will rest upon him; but if not, it will return to you. And stay in that house, eating and drinking what they give you; for the labourer is worthy of his wages. Do not keep moving from house to house. And*

*whatever city you enter, and they receive you, eat what is set before you; and heal those in it who are sick, and say to them,* ***'The kingdom of God has come near to you.'*** Luke 10:2-9. (Author's emphasis)

They had to go and do the same as their Master. I often wonder what the disciples were saying to each other as they prepared for this adventure. I am sending you as lambs among wolves, Jesus had told them. They probably would have preferred not to have known that! Great – hands up who wants to go into that howling pack! But they carry the same power, and the same bringing down of the kingdom is seen, as they go out with faith in the Lord's direction. They returned from their trip excitedly. It had happened – that same kingdom had invaded the situations that they had faced. They had not been ripped apart by wolves after all. 'Lord, even the demons are subject to Your name' was their report. Jesus responds by saying: Yes, I saw Satan fall like lightening. In other words there has just been a clash of kingdoms, and guess who has won.

After His death and resurrection, prior to Jesus returning to heaven, He instructed His disciples to continue to do what He had been doing. In fact He promised them that they would do greater things than He had done, because when He returned to His Father, He would release the Holy Spirit to come and dwell in and among them permanently.

*'Truly, truly, I say to you, he who believes in Me, the works that I do shall he do also,* ***and greater works than these shall he do*** *because I go to the Father. And whatever you ask in My name, that will I do, that the Father may be glorified in the Son. If you ask Me anything in My name, I will do it. If you love Me, you will keep My commandments, and I will ask the Father, and He will give you another Helper, that He may be with you forever'.* John 14:12-16.

*'..... but* ***you shall receive power*** *when the Holy Spirit has come upon you, and you shall be My witnesses both in Jerusalem, and in all Judea and Samaria, and even to the remotest part of the earth.'* Acts. 1:8. (Author's emphases)

The book of Acts is a dramatic testimony to the fact that under the powerful anointing of the Holy Spirit, like Jesus, they moved out in faith on what God was telling them to do. Here was the kingdom of heaven powerfully invading culture and society wherever the people of God were to be found. We see the realm of the impossible invading the natural realm. Lame men walking. Prison doors opening. Powerful demonstrations of healing. Dead being brought back to life. Thousands born again and reproducing themselves. Here were ordinary men and women, hearing what God was saying, and moving out in mountain moving faith and turning the world upside down.

Might it just be that the people of God would again begin to realise their divine and powerful calling? Might it just be that what Jesus started, and the apostles pursued, arise in the people of God again? Might it be that God will again arise and scatter His enemies. Might it just be that some dry bones will hear the Word of the Lord and rise up as a mighty army with conquering faith? Might it just be – you and I? It would not be the first time. All down the years, especially in times of revival, people have believed God in faith and witnessed the impossible becoming possible.

Faith that is rooted in God's promises is an invincible force:

*'And I also say to you that you are Peter, and upon this rock I will build My church, and the gates of Hades shall not overpower it. I will give you the keys of the kingdom of heaven; and whatever you shall bind on earth shall be bound in heaven, and whatever you shall loose on earth shall be loosed in heaven.'* Matthew 16:18-19.

Peter was given a full revelation of who Jesus was. God revealed something to Peter, that in spite of his weaknesses and failures, would never leave him. The word of God became to him a revelation. Jesus was saying to Peter, 'You have just seen and heard something from God, and on that revelation I will build something that the very gates of hell itself will not be able to prevail against. Jesus also promises a locking and unlocking of the kingdom which would affect earth.

## Chapter 13

# Faith that Unlocks Doors

~ God will increasingly use us to touch some of His lost sheep if we are available. ***Availability*** is the secret to a fulfilled life of miracles ~

~ Faith unlocks doors for us, both natural and spiritual, that we would not ever have thought possible in our wildest imaginings ~

I am going to share two stories. The first illustrates how God will use simple faith to reach the need of one of His lost sheep, no matter what door is locked against it. The second, a testimony of provision from the world's locked storehouse.

During the period that I was in general medical practice, I inherited a patient in her late twenties who we will call Sue, although that was not her real name. Sue had married a heroin addict several years before, who had become born again through one of the men in our church who had befriended him. Sadly this young man, Sue's husband, had been found dead in another city in unsolved suspicious circumstances, nearly two years before I met Sue. Sue herself had subsequently become a heroin addict. She and her husband had had a daughter, who at the time of this account was about six years of age. Sue was living in a council flat and unable to work due to her addiction. She looked after her child very well, who was always spotlessly clean, immaculately dressed, and regularly attended her junior school. I came to know Sue well as she attended my surgery on many occasions for support for herself, and for her lovely little girl who suffered with ear infections on a fairly regular basis.

I had chatted to Sue about the Lord and His ability to set her free from addiction and give her a full life again, which in measure her deceased husband had found. She always listened – I suppose she had to if she wanted my support! – but never appeared to want to take things forward in terms of discovering the future that God intended for her.

One day as I had finished a busy morning surgery, and was looking forward to going home to lunch for some relaxation before my later afternoon session, I distinctly heard the Lord tell me to go and visit Sue. I remember having one of those pointless discussions with the Lord, about how inconvenient it was, and it was three miles away, and what if she was not there, and I had just seen twenty-eight needy people already, and did not I deserve a break? The Lord remained silent, and was clearly not up for discussing the matter of my needs at that time, or my objections! I knew I had to obey, and so I got in my car and drove to her address.

I arrived to receive no reply to my knocking, and looking through the letterbox there were no evident lights on inside her rather dark flat, or any sign of occupation. I pushed and banged the door loudly again and called through the letterbox. No reply was forthcoming. I turned away from the door into the landing area and with my back to the door, said something along these lines: 'Lord You have brought me here for a purpose to see Sue, so I now need You to open that door for me because I cannot get in!' Isn't it funny how we sometimes furnish the Lord with information He already was fully aware of before we were even born! Sometimes I think He must get rather tired of His children telling Him things that are plainly obvious! I turned back around to find the door now slightly ajar, with still no sound of life within the interior. There had been no sound of anyone unbolting the door from within. 'Thank You Lord, that is helpful, as I do not have a warrant for breaking and entering!' I ventured into the hallway, calling Sue's name. Eventually I heard a muffled response from one of the bedrooms at the far end of the flat.

There lay Sue in a darkened room, shrouded in bedding, looking awful and probably still sleeping off the effects of a fix the night before. I assured her as to who I was, and asked if it was alright to put the light on. She gazed at me wide eyed and asked how on earth I had got into the flat, as she had not only dead-locked the door but double bolted it both at the top and the bottom. I asked if she had heard my knocking and calling, and she affirmed that she had.

However, she said that she had no intention whatsoever of letting the caller in as she was sure it was an official come to talk to her about her rent arrears!

I told her exactly why I had come and what had happened. Now her eyes were even wider. I went on to share with her about God's passionate love for her, and how He wanted to rescue her from her life of self-abuse, and shared the gospel with her again. She told me that she had grown up in a Roman Catholic family, and that she did have a bible, which, as I recall she was able to produce. I prayed with her and as I left she examined her undamaged door with a shake of her head and a look of total unbelief.

I would like to say that she gave her life to Christ, was soundly delivered, and is now serving the Lord somewhere. I cannot say that, as I was never to see Sue again. Soon after this incident the Lord led me to resign from that practice and move to another part of the country. But for all I know she may today be serving the Lord, and I may meet her again. It would not be the first time that I have heard of such things happening.

However, that was not the point of the story, but rather it was this. If we will be open to the voice of God at all times, and respond to what He is saying - even perhaps sometimes reluctantly, as in my case - and go out in faith on the word, then God will quite easily cut through the obstacles and impossibilities that stand in the way of His purposes. It is very fulfilling and exciting when we move with Him in faith in these ways. Our Christian lives take on fresh meaning and purpose. Faith really does unlock doors for us, not only natural ones, but doors in the spiritual realm too that we would probably not even have dreamed of or thought possible in all our wildest imaginings.

I mentioned earlier in the book about some of the situations that faced me as I contemplated the decision as to whether to accept the place in medical school that God had opened up to me. One of these was over the provision of finance for the whole six years of training. I had enjoyed a regular secure salary, and now I was faced with living on a local authority grant which was less than half of what I had been earning. This second story concerns a visit by a council grant official, who I am sure are there to see fairness in the allocation of funds, but were known to operate very strictly within their written parameters.

Following my grant having been settled and approved, my wife, Jeanne, one afternoon had a totally unexpected visit from one of these officials, who we learnt, had been allocated to our case. He apparently had been looking through our application and noted that we had not made any claims for various allowances that were, unknown to us, available to help defray some of our children's schooling expenses. Items such as school uniforms and shoes, school meals, school educational trips and other items were payable in addition to the basic grant. This was available for what was euphemistically termed 'mature students' to which appellation I apparently fitted! We subsequently learnt that it was fully our responsibility to make any claim, but was one of those situations that unless you had happened to receive a prophetic word from someone you would have never known that such funds were available. We had not received any prophecy! So entirely out of character, and with no need whatsoever to do so, this kind man drove from his office to our house to discuss the matter with us. If that were not amazing enough, after he had gone through all of our income and expenditure he found that we fell a few pounds above the minimum income line to receive this extra grant. Instead of appearing relieved that his council funds would not be further jeopardised by us, Jeanne told me he appeared most upset, and said 'Surely there must be some other expenditure we could find to entitle you to this money.' Jeanne telephoned me, and I could think of nothing that would qualify as an 'expense', although I mentioned an unofficial arrangement I had at the time with my father on some money he had loaned me, but I was sure that would not count as there was no paperwork which documented it. She relayed this to the official, whose eyes immediately lit up, included it in his figures, and obtained this generous grant for us for the rest of my course. I have to say in all the years since that event, I have never ever had a government official bending over backwards to find an excuse to give me money, and when he has, leave my house with such delight! Have you?

I could relate many more miracles of Father's provision for us during those years. Food would sometimes just arrive on the doorstep, we had no idea where from and by whom. Money would come in plain envelopes through the letter box. One couple purchased us a new sewing machine to enable Jeanne to make clothes for our children. In the first three years of the course when I had the normal university vacations, I used this time to service and repair people's cars and other engineering ventures. I always ended up with more work than I could cope with, and began to wonder why I had not started a business in that line years before! During my later clinical years, when I was trying to supplement my grant in this way, my fellow church leaders, in seeing that I was attempting far too much, very kindly gave me an allowance so that I did not need to pursue that any more. All these wonderful miraculous provisions of a gracious Father, through the kindness of His saints, as well as very possibly angels, are far too many to detail here.

I still to this day shake my head in wonderment, and am reminded of King Darius who virtually gave Ezra the keys to the royal mint, and told him to help himself to what was needed to rebuild the city of Jerusalem. Not quite the sort of thing that kings are generally known for, especially in those days. God unlocks treasury doors for His children when needed, if they will walk by faith, and not sight.

# CHAPTER 14

# FAITH THAT POSSESSES

~ Faith is the vehicle through which God's truth becomes a life changing reality, and that enables us to be possessors of our God-appointed promises and inheritance ~

~ God's truth is there to change us. It is not there to be admired like fine porcelain in a display cabinet! ~

When God created the earth for the residence and blessing of His pinnacle of creation, humankind, Adam and Eve were destined to bring the earth under their godly rule, and possess and enjoy the increasing abundance that the earth would produce. We know only too well the story, inasmuch that Eve, deceived by Satan, and followed by Adam, were robbed of all this by their disobedience. We really see their failure to let that instructional word of God to them become the undergirding of all the hope that lay before them. When the enemy questioned God's word to them, they listened to that instead of what God had told them. They failed to take humankind's first step of faith, refute Satan's lie and begin to possess the earth.

Hebrews 11 cites Abel, Enoch and Noah as three men that began to move in faith following that dreadful debacle, but it is to Abraham that God promises that he would become an inheritor of the whole world - that which Adam and Eve lost by disobedience. While they had dropped the baton, through faith Abraham was to pick it up again and run with it, becoming an inheritor of God's blessings. Possessions that God had already prepared for him, were actually to become his, but that would only happen by a decisive act of Abraham's trust in God's spoken promises. He was to become an 'heir to the world.' God promised Abraham that he would be the father of many nations when he and his wife were childless and both totally past the possibility of producing a single child, as we have already seen. I am now going to quote several passages of scripture which I would encourage you to read carefully as they are very instructive in the matter of you and I possessing God's promises.

*'For the promise to Abraham or to his descendants that he would be heir of the world was not through the Law, but* ***through the righteousness of faith.'*** Romans 4:13. (Author's emphasis)

*Now the Lord said to Abram, 'Go forth from your country, and from your relatives and from your father's house, to the land which I will show you, and I will make you a great nation, and I will bless you, and make your name great, and so you shall be a blessing, and I will bless those who bless you, and the one who curses you I will curse, and in you all the families of the earth shall be blessed.'* Genesis 12:1-3.

*'And I will establish My covenant between Me and you, And I will multiply you exceedingly.' And Abram fell on his face, and God talked with him, saying, 'As for Me, behold, My covenant is with you, And you shall be the father of a multitude of nations. No longer shall your name be called Abram, but your name shall be Abraham, for I will make you the father of a multitude of nations. And I will make you exceedingly fruitful, and I will make nations of you, and kings shall come forth from you. And I will establish My covenant between Me and you and your descendants after you throughout their generations for an everlasting covenant, to be God to you and to your descendants after you.* ***And I will give to you*** *and to your descendants after you, the land of your sojournings,* ***all the land of Canaan, for an everlasting possession,*** *and I will be their God.'* Genesis 17:2-8. (Author's emphasis)

It is very important to notice that in speaking about Abraham's blessings, Paul makes it clear that we who 'are of faith' can be likewise blessed. Faith is the conduit through which God can pour His blessings into our lives and out to others. Abraham's faith released a flow of God's blessing out to everyone else.

> *'Even so Abraham believed God, and it was reckoned to him as righteousness. Therefore, be sure that it is those who are of faith who are sons of Abraham. And the Scripture, foreseeing that God would justify the Gentiles by faith, preached the gospel beforehand to Abraham, saying, 'All the nations shall be blessed in you' So then those who are of faith are blessed with Abraham, the believer.... Now that no one is justified by the Law before God is evident; for, **'The righteous man shall live by faith.'** However, the Law is not of faith; on the contrary, 'He who practices them shall live by them.' Christ redeemed us from the curse of the Law, having become a curse for us-- for it is written, 'Cursed is everyone who hangs on a tree'-- **in order that in Christ Jesus the blessing of Abraham might come to the Gentiles, so that we might receive the promise of the Spirit through faith.'*** Galatians 3:6-14. (Author's emphasis)

Paul contrasts the inability of the Law, and the curse accruing from failure to keep it, with faith that releases blessing through the work of Christ, ***'in order that...the blessing of Abraham might come to the Gentiles!'*** So through Abraham's faith, we have the opportunity of possessing all that God has for ***us***, through his example. We need to understand the vast potential that faith releases.

We also see that while Abraham became the possessor of an incalculable inheritance, interestingly his eye was on another goal:

> *'By faith he lived as an alien in the land of promise, as in a foreign land, dwelling in tents with Isaac and Jacob, fellow heirs of the same promise; for **he was looking for the city which has foundations,** whose architect and builder is God.'* Hebrews 11:9-10. (Author's emphasis)

He was looking for a city, the city of God. I would have liked to ask him: 'But Abraham you have surely inherited lots of cities, why are you looking for another one?' I think he may have said something like: 'Ah, yes, but this one is different, this is an eternal city. God's city!' Do you see what faith had accomplished in this old man who had everything that the world of his time could offer? His eye of faith is on the real goal. He never saw it with his natural eyes, but I am pretty sure that this eternal city was more real to him by his eyes of faith, than the earthly cities that he inherited in the physical lands that God gave to him, and that he would have seen with his natural eyes.
The person of faith while appreciating the natural order around them, has visualised something beyond and eternal, that they will give their lives for.

Paul echoed this same conviction and far seeing vision, and lived out his life of faith in much the same way:

> *'Brethren, I do not regard myself as having laid hold of it yet; but one thing I do: forgetting what lies behind and* ***reaching forward to what lies ahead, I press on toward the goal*** *for the prize of the upward call of God in Christ Jesus. Let us therefore, as many as are perfect, have this attitude; and if in anything you have a different attitude, God will reveal that also to you.'* Philippians 3:13-15. (Author's emphasis)

How does this apply to us today? Are we called to inherit by faith? Do we have any promises to lay hold of? I come across many Christians today who live in spiritual poverty, often with little sense of purpose or direction. The truth of the believer's inheritance in Christ, or taking hold of their spiritual possessions, is met with astonishment that such things might exist for the twenty-first century Christian.
The writer of Hebrews enjoins us 'not to be sluggish, but to be imitators of those who through faith and patience inherit the

promises'. (Heb.6:12). The scriptures are full of the promises of God that are there for us to inherit and possess, but they are appropriated by active faith in what God has promised.

My mother, over many years, collected a beautiful set of Royal Crown Derby 'Blue and Gold' pattern bone china piece by piece. From my earliest memories it resided in a glass fronted china cabinet. I can only recall one occasion where it was actually used for the purpose it was made, and only then under threat of certain death if anyone dared to harm it in any way. On my mother's death, my wife and I inherited it. You will probably have no problem guessing where it now resides! On special shelves in our dining area where it sits in all its resplendent glory - and is never used, of course. It just sits there to be admired and regularly washed and dusted! Then when we go off to glory one of our children will no doubt take possession of it, and put it in a china cabinet.......! How crazy you say, and you are absolutely right. While the china is a beautiful work of craftsmanship and art, and because of that, it probably has great worth in a collectors eyes, it is in practical terms non-functional. However we daily use a collection of what I can only call 'mongrel' crockery. Two cups and saucers from one set, four from another, cereal bowls from three other sets. Dinner plates from two different sets, and so on. Most of the pieces from these original complete sets have long since ended in the waste bin due to a series of sad accidents! I am sure our family is not unique in such things. The point of the story is to illustrate accurately what we as believers so often end up doing with our Father's 'exceedingly great and precious promises' (2 Peter 1:4)

I often hear of Christians getting together in homes all across the country for bible studies, and churches becoming popular venues because the minister, pastor or leader preaches the word of God in great 'depth', or conferences being attended where some renowned bible teacher is in the country. There is very much to be commended by such activities, so please do not misunderstand me. I love studying the scriptures. I love receiving good teaching from the Word of God. I love conferences where some gifted biblical teacher is preaching. But sometimes in my inimitable way I ask of those attending such venues, what they actually have learnt over the past twelve months that has radically changed their lives. What truth of scripture has become such a revelation to them that they have had to change their minds, and subsequently, their ways, on an issue. What promise of God have they discovered that has transformed their relationship with Jesus. Sadly, many times I either get that look of panic of someone feeling cornered, or a look that is really saying 'What sort of a dumb question is that supposed to be?'

Of course God's word is to be highly prized, studied, taught and treasured, but if we never, through the process of faith that we have been describing, get it working in our lives in such a way that it invokes ongoing changes - if we never take the promises of scripture, make them ours and get them operational – or if we never realise that God has given us a rich spiritual inheritance to possess and enjoy in this life, as well as that to come, then it is exactly like the 'Blue and Gold' china sitting all of its life on display, but never used for the purpose for which it was produced.

Faith is the vehicle through which God's truth becomes a vital and life changing reality, and that enables us to be possessors of our God-appointed promises and inheritance.

# Chapter 15

# Staying the Course

~ Faith always grows under pressure ~

~ Too often as God's children, we settle for second best because we will not fix our hearts firmly into what God has instructed and promised ~

I have met many Christians over the years who recount to me something that God has spoken into them in the past. Something that came to them at that time as a 'now' living word, and which inspired faith within them. However it had, over the years, become dry and dead, and they were now only going through the motions of the past. Why? Has God forgotten what He said to them? Of course not, as we cannot attribute to God a failing memory! In fact God made it very clear through Isaiah that His Word has within itself the inherent power to bring about fully that which it declares:

> *'For as the rain and the snow come down from heaven, and do not return there without watering the earth, and making it bear and sprout, and furnishing seed to the sower and bread to the eater; So shall My word be which goes forth from My mouth;* ***It shall not return to Me empty, without accomplishing what I desire, and without succeeding in the matter for which I sent it.'*** Isaiah 55:10-11 (Author's emphasis)

The word of God will always succeed in the matter for which it was sent out. When God makes a declaration of what He ***will*** do, then He always does it without fail. For instance when God said through the prophet Joel: ***'I will pour out My Spirit on all mankind, and your sons and daughters will prophesy, your old men will dream dreams, your young men will see visions',*** He did just that. It had no bearing on whether anyone believed it would happen or whether they were convinced it would not happen – on the day of Pentecost it happened anyway.

It matters little whether you believe that God's glory is going to cover the whole earth ***'as the waters cover the sea'***, because its fulfilment will certainly take place whether we believe it and become involved in the process, or not. At God's appointed time it will occur!

However, there is another profound truth that we have to grasp. It is that God calls us as His sons to work together with Him in the fulfilment of His purposes here on earth. That was His call to Adam and Eve, but they choose not to obey the Lord's word. Now in Christ, God has restored to us that place of being co-labourers with Him again. That is a tremendous privilege that carries major responsibility. Did Abraham have the choice not to leave his home city and launch out with God. For sure he did. God's promises to him were based on Abraham's deep settled trust in God and His word, and his launching out in faith upon it. All the promises flowed from that. Abraham had the option not to listen and obey, and there would have been no record of him having become our father in the faith!

When God called me to give up my career and go and study medicine, did I have a choice? Yes of course I did. I could either launch out in faith and obey His Word, or stay as I was, in the security of what I knew worked within the sphere of my human wisdom and past experience. It was not until my will became aligned with His will, that the miracles started to happen, and the purposes of God for my life at that time began to be fulfilled.

Jesus told a parable that is recorded in all the first three gospels. It is generally called the parable of the sower, although I personally believe it is better called the parable of the Seed and the Soil. Jesus makes it clear in Mark 4:13 that if we do not understand this parable, then we will not understand any of them. I puzzled over this statement for a long time, and it made me more inquisitive in my study of it. You may already be asking what on earth this parable has to do with faith, and the matter of living words given to us by the Lord which have died within our experience. I believe this parable gives some answers to that question.

The disciples, having realised there was perhaps something more behind the story than was immediately obvious, come to Jesus for some revelation and instruction. Jesus, in response begins to open up the deeper and hidden meaning of the parable following the disciple's enquiry. I find that God always responds to the enquirer, whereas the uninterested and inattentive will miss vital truth. Jesus explains that the sower sows the 'seed' which is the word of the kingdom. (Compare Mk.4:14 and Matt.13:19.) This is the word of God being sent forth by God into the heart 'soil' of its hearers. The issue from now on is not about the seed, but the soil. The ***seed*** will be perfect – it will always germinate and produce fruit provided it has the right environment, because it is the eternally living word of God. The issue now is all about the ***heart response of the hearer*** to the word that has been sown into it. In three cases the soil, for one reason or another, fails to produce fruit. Only in the case of one of the soils is there a fruitful harvest:

> *'And the seed in the* ***good soil,*** *these are the ones who have heard the word in an honest and good heart, and hold it fast, and bear fruit with perseverance.'* Luke 8:15. (Author's emphasis)

In other words they are people who give great attention to the word they hear. They value it because of its source. It is not 'in one ear and out of the other.' Jesus, when telling this parable, identifies people who 'Have ears, but do not hear', and therefore tells His disciples to 'take care ***how*** they hear'! Those with 'good heart' soil 'hold it fast' – they do not let it go, and the fruit comes as a result of 'perseverance.' This is the ongoing practical application of the word that they have heard into their daily lives.

We live in a culture of the 'instant' and easy quick fix. There have been many advantages that have accrued to humankind from this. However, there are also some negative aspects which often leave us very lacking in the areas of patience, persistence, perseverance, seeking, searching out, diligence, waiting, and application. If the Lord gives us a word, we want the outcome now, or preferably sooner! We would think the farmer who finished sowing his field with wheat on Monday, and arriving in the same field the following Tuesday morning with his combine harvester fuelled up and ready to go had somehow lost it! We all know there is a process between sowing the seed and reaping the harvest, and time is necessary for those processes to take place.

You will recall my story of the wood stain in Chapter 8. My tins of stain from the USA took several weeks to materialize. Why? I have no idea, but to me that was not the issue. God told me He would supply, and I knew He would. That was the bottom line. People of course were asking me when? - I could not answer that, because He had not told me. I just had the assurance He ***would,*** and I was content to leave the '***when'*** with Him, and my decoration plans had to wait. I remember that with the wait, the word, and the assurance that I had in it, grew stronger in me. The more people asked if it had arrived, the more I became convinced that it would, which when you think of it seems back the front. But in my experience faith grows under pressure, because you are pushed further and further into God and His word to you. It is similar to that which Abraham experienced over the promise of Isaac. It states in Romans 4:19-20 that he ***'did not waver in unbelief, but grew strong in faith'*** in respect to the promise of God, even after fully reviewing the impossibilities of it all.

My wife Jeanne is a keen gardener, and has over the years gained much experience in plants. On many occasions I have seen what to me looks like a few dead sticks poking out of the ground, or a plant that previously has been healthy and in growth that has now apparently died. I make comments like, 'Well, that was a waste of money', or 'Why do you not dig that up and plant something else? She will just say, 'No, I have learnt to leave things like that alone, because down in the roots there is probably still life.' As I write this, there is a plant that I had pronounced death and destruction over several times, that much to my chagrin has, after a whole season of apparent mortification, sprung to life again and is putting out leaves in all directions! Too often we fail to hold on fast to the word the Lord gives us. We fail to persevere with it.

Referring back to the parable about the seed and the soil, the enemy comes and steals God's word from the hardened surface of our hearts, or we run with it for a while, but when we do not see immediate answers, and the heat is turned up by external forces, we let it wither and die in us. Alternatively, we let three 'counter-words' or weeds, that the enemy sows in our thinking, take root in our hearts. Jesus outlined these as the cares of the world, the love for riches, and the lust for other things, all of which choke out the good seed of the word that has been sown in us.

I believe that our Father is wanting and willing to use us in the revelation and power of His kingdom here on earth, far more than we are ready to embrace that call. He 'sows' the word of the kingdom into us, and looks for a harvest. It all has to do with His will being done on earth, even as it is being done in heaven right now. His word comes into my heart, and I embrace it and persevere with it, and put my faith in it. Through that, something of the kingdom of God, God's divine rule, is manifested on earth.

You may well have thought 'What on earth has a certain stain product to decorate your house with, got to do with the kingdom of God coming to earth?' or 'What on earth has God giving you a place in medical school, and taking you through the course to successful completion, got to do with His will in heaven being done on earth?' Another fallacy that we can embrace, is that of only associating the working of God with 'church' and with what we may perceive are 'spiritual' outcomes. This for many years was exactly my own perception. However, this is entirely false. What was the 'point' of the cursing of the fig tree, or Peter getting the tax dues from the fish's mouth, or was that just Jesus wasting His time? Naturally we would refute that suggestion, but would look deeper into the scenarios to begin to learn the spiritual lessons that were contained in them.

For me, the two instances from my own life that I have just cited have had very clear 'kingdom' implications. Firstly they enlarged my capacity to believe God for the impossible, and thus to exercise my faith 'muscles' for further challenges. Secondly, they became a powerful testimony of faith to those with whom I shared these things. I suggest that even as you read of them, your level of faith will be challenged and encouraged. Thirdly, it teaches that the word of God can be activated by faith into ***all*** areas of our lives, and destroys this sacred/secular divide that so limits the workings of the Spirit of God into the earth by the people of God.

So often we can miss the blessing through our impatience and lack of persistence. There are times when it is almost as if there is a clock ticking towards some deadline. There appears no evident fulfilment of what God has promised as the deadline gets nearer and nearer! I call these God's 11.59 moments! We tend always to link faith with time.

I recall an incident when we were moving from one part of the UK to another, that was over a hundred miles away. We had heard God clearly speak to us and knew He was requiring us to make the move. The timing appeared wrong in so many ways. It was not a good time in respect of our children's education, especially as they were all at excellent schools. It was very disappointing in terms of my medical career, as I was just on the verge of becoming the senior partner of the general medical practice that I was working in. I had prayed for several years for this, as my desire was to have a practice that was under my direction and that had a clear Christian foundation and ethic, and would be a real place of healing in the full biblical sense of the word. We also had just finished altering and restoring our home after about six years of hard work. However, we knew this was God's direction and right timing which was being confirmed by our fellow church leaders at that period. Accordingly we began to search for a new home in the town that the Lord had made it very clear that we were to live. This we expected would be easy and plain sailing as we were after all pursuing the will of God. This proved to be our first wrong assumption. We could not locate any home that suited our needs. It seemed that all property for sale had dried up especially just for us!

The weeks past and the deadline for getting moved for the start of the children's autumn school term loomed large. Then we came across a house in a village some three miles from the town in which we were searching. It seemed to fit the bill, had everything we needed and at a price we could afford. However, it was not in the town of God's choosing. We of course tried to rationalise the situation and persuade ourselves that it was near enough. After all Lord we are desperate. As we prayed for guidance on this, the Lord spoke into our spirits and said 'You can have that house if you want it, and I will bless you there, but it is second best,' and He said no more! Well we are now in a dilemma. Our house sale was on the verge of falling through because we could not give a completion date. We have no new home to move to, and what we thought we had is second best.

I remember thinking that so often as the children of God, we end up with second best because we will not fix our hearts firmly into what God has instructed, promised, and is leading us towards. Instead of waiting, we feel we need to take matters into out own hands. Bad move! We fail to use the Word of God as that which '***is the underlying immovable rock-like structure that turns hope into complete certainty, and gives concrete and irrefutable proof that what we are unable to perceive with our natural senses, is in fact***

***real and fully in existence'*** and wait for the miracle to happen. I will develop this further in the next chapter.

With some apprehension, I have to say, we turned our 'second best' house down. The following weekend I had come to preach in the church that God was calling us to. We were invited for lunch at a couple's home from that church, and who were fully aware of our need. After lunch as we were sitting relaxing, the wife of the couple casually picked up the local newspaper and was looking through the 'Houses for Sale' private advertisements. Most of you will be aware that estate agents (realtors) use big spread page adverts, and we had been scanning these for weeks, as well as going to estate agent offices regularly. However, tucked away in one of the small printed columns was a simple two or three line private advertisement for a new house that was being built in the town that we were to live. There were hardly any details, but we felt we should follow it up. We contacted the vendor who was a builder, and were encouraged enough to visit the site. On a site adjacent was a two hundred year old cottage which was clearly being developed and enlarged. My wife took one look at it, and said to the builder that this was exactly what she would love – was it for sale? While the builder had planned this as a later project, seeing a potential sale, agreed not only to sell it to us, but to divert his efforts from the new house he was building to completing the cottage. We knew immediately in our hearts that this was the house that God had planned for us all along, and that this was His best.

It would be an understatement to say that the next three months were traumatic as we wrestled with builders, resale of our current home as the first sale had dropped through, sorting out the children's schooling and so on. The details are too complex to pursue here, but through it all we had the full assurance that we were in the centre of God's best for us. As I look back on the fifteen years that we lived in that home, I have to say that they were some of the happiest years of my life, and often think how easy it would have been to have missed

God's best through impatience and the pressing circumstances that seem to force us to take matters into our own hands and 'help God out'.

As for the Christian practice that I had prayed for, and had had to leave behind, a medical colleague from another practice and another church who was looking for change, took my place, and some twelve months after my leaving, developed it in the way I had envisioned and had been hoping and praying to do myself. Thus God took care of that detail too.

## Chapter 16

# Why the Delay?

~ God will test us, not to gain further knowledge about us, but rather that ***we*** can gain further knowledge about ***ourselves!*** ~

~ You can have anointing, but without the development of character and faith, like King Saul, you will likely fail ~

For many years in my adventure of faith, I was often puzzled as to why, when it seemed that God had spoken so clearly about an issue, nothing appeared to happen, or circumstances, far from opening up towards what God was saying, actually appeared to close down. At times it even seemed that all hell had broken loose to prevent me moving forward and into what God had promised. Often in sharing with other Christians who were seeking to operate in this life of faith, they would report the same or similar things. Probably many of you reading this will have also had these experiences, and know exactly what I am referring to. Sadly, I have had Christian friends over the years who have had several significant disappointments of this nature, would say that as a result they are now no longer walking with God in any way. There are others who I know, that have pulled back from an active life of faith in the Word of God.

I will give you an example from my own life. A few years ago the Lord made it clear to my wife and I that we were to move to another city to be part of the local church there. We sought the Lord as to where we should live and after several weeks found a suitable property to purchase. We were convinced that our own house was at that time very saleable, mainly because of the type of house that it was, with its quiet location and stunning views across open country, which afforded all around us lovely rural walks. The house market in the town was brisk with many more buyers than sellers at that time. We were fully convinced that our house would be snapped up. On contacting several estate agents to estimate its value, all of them agreed the house would sell immediately and were clamouring for us to let them market our property. We felt we were 'on a roll' with the

Lord in all this, and so on this basis, and against all reasoned and sensible practice, made an offer on the new house we had found and wanted to purchase. This was subsequently accepted on the condition that we completed the purchase in three months. We felt fully at peace in our spirits to move forward on this agreement, convinced that this period was more than enough time to sell our existing property.

I recall my solicitor, who was a Christian, asking me if I was being wise. He also strongly advised me that as the house I was buying was over one hundred years old, I should obtain a full structural survey. I told him I was not being wise at all, and in 'expert' eyes was being utterly foolish, and by the way I would not spend several hundred pounds on a structural survey as I would still buy the house whatever the report, because this was the one Father had shown us to purchase! I really did appreciate his concern and professionalism and my brain agreed with him, but my spirit did not! We were not to be moved.

At the end of three months we had not had a single offer on our home, or even much in the way of interested folks coming to view it. The estate agent we had instructed had no explanation for this, and he was completely baffled. Everything was going against all the prevailing market trends and expectations. We began to realize we were experiencing another miracle of God – that against all odds, our house was ***not*** selling when everything shouted at us that it should be! Our estate agent could only suggest we reduced the price, which we did not feel was right. By now we were required to complete on our new home, and had to take out a one hundred percent loan to purchase it as agreed. Even at that stage we were still expecting the imminent sale of our home. Three ***years*** later our home finally sold, with the consequent cost of our bridging loan for that extended period. Friends had kindly prayed for us, believed for us, prophesied over us, and even a group had come and prayed around the house. In the end it was clear that they were too embarrassed to ask us any more if the house had sold as the months continued to go by.

How did we cope with all that? It is necessary to bear in mind that we had learnt something of the ways of God, and in walking in confidence in God's word and promises. It would be wrong to give the impression that we did not have the occasional moments of questioning and frustrations, especially as we were fully convinced we were pursuing that which God had asked us to do. We knew we were not in disobedience! However, for the most part of those three years, we remained confident in the knowledge that God is good at all times, and all that was happening was firmly in His hands. Father was working it all together for our good, and all we were required to do was trust Him, regardless of the outward circumstances. He also gave us a promise from Jeremiah 29:11: ***'For I know the plans that I have for you,' declares the LORD, 'plans for welfare and not for calamity to give you a future and a hope.'*** While we knew this verse was quite out of its context, God spoke this into our hearts time and time again, and we used to regularly pray it back to Him. It served to thicken the 'concrete' that we were standing on!

I know God does not delight in seeing us squirm as the pressure to wait heightens or as the deadlines draw nearer. I am convinced of God's constant love for us, and of His inherent faithfulness and goodness that never changes. He will never act out of any other purpose than for our blessing. After all, those 'deadlines' are only ***our*** perception of the situation. We sometimes tell God in these situations that He really does not understand. We need the money ***now***. We really do need that situation to change ***now***. We really do need to have a clear decision ***now***. We totally forget that God clearly sees the whole of our lives from start to finish, and therefore has a life encompassing perspective that we can never have. What did we learn from those three years of waiting? Verses that we all know only too well took on more than superficial meaning for us:

*'We know that God causes all things to work together for good to those who love God'* Romans 8:28.

*'Cease striving and know that I am God'* Psalm 46:10.

*'...being confident of this, that He who began a good work in you will carry it on to completion...'* Philippians 1:6.

*'For you have need of endurance, so that when you have done the will of God, you may receive what was promised.'* Hebrews 10:36.

*'...imitators of those who through faith and patience inherit the promises.'* Hebrews 6:12.

Was God teasing me, or playing tricks? Not at all, but seeking to mature me in my walk of faith. How else could my 'faith muscles' develop? If God had continued to deal with me in His school of faith in the way He did in those early days of my journey into medial school, when He answered all my questions, and provided for my needs immediately, how would I have ever learnt to trust Him in greater challenges and bigger steps of faith and obedience to His word? God was testing me, not so that He would gain more knowledge of me. He knew all that in fine detail already, but rather that I could gain knowledge about ***myself***. There were the frequent taunts of the enemy during those years of 'has God said?'. The occasional circumstantial frustrations, and even at times the well meaning questions of family and friends, all would conspire to try to make you doubt the word and the love of God. But through them all, one learns increasingly each time to press even more firmly into the unshakable Rock on which our lives are being lived out.

I must tell you the end of the story. The three year delay did have very positive aspects. It enabled us to refurbish the whole of the interior of the new house and make a temporary study in the loft space, thus avoiding living daily in the mess and chaos that all this work would have entailed. Also this new house that we had purchased three years previously had increased in value by about seventy percent due to huge price inflation in that particular area of the country, whereas prices in the area of our old house had hardly moved in the same period. This meant a very significant cost advantage to us, which covered the interest paid on the bridging loan several times over. We came out in profit! We were blessed in the development of our character and faith, which was perhaps more important. God certainly is in debt to no man, and His perspectives are so different and all-encompassing from ours!

Sadly, we often cannot bear the delays, 'chicken out' and try to help God out of what we perceive is a predicament. King Saul is a classic example of this to his eventual complete downfall. He had been selected by God to be Israel's first king at the unwise request of the nation. From all accounts he was a wholesome and handsome young man, appears rather more shy than pushy and arrogant. God gives him a new heart and a powerful anointing of the Holy Spirit, a wholehearted response and affirmation from the people and an initial great victory in war. Somewhat later, faced with a military challenge by Israel's arch enemies the Philistines, and needing to wait for the prophet Samuel to arrive to conduct the burnt offering in which the Lord's favour was sought at times of battle, he became impatient because he perceived that the outward circumstances were changing against him. Samuel was delayed in his arrival, so Saul contrary to the word of God through the prophet, offered the burnt offering himself. He clearly felt that God was obviously not aware of the pressing circumstances and that he needed to get things moving! When Samuel eventually did arrive, this was his response:

> *'And Samuel said to Saul, 'You have acted foolishly; you have not kept the commandment of the Lord your God, which He commanded you, for now the Lord would have established your kingdom over Israel forever. But now your kingdom*

*shall not endure. The Lord has sought out for Himself a man after His own heart, and the Lord has appointed him as ruler over His people, because you have not kept what the Lord commanded you.'* 1 Samuel 13:13-14.

This incident was clearly the beginning of the slow but sure demise of a man who had everything from God that he needed to pursue a powerful and godly reign – except character and faith. It makes very sad reading.

In contrast, we can observe the shepherd boy David, similarly anointed by the prophet Samuel to eventually succeed king Saul. At David's anointing we are told that the spirit of the Lord came powerfully on David from that day forward. (1 Samuel 16:13), hardly an event he would miss or fail to understand. I am quite sure it was the talk of the whole family in the years that followed, as to when David was going to take the throne. I am sure it would frequently be in David's mind too. As the story unfolds, David has to face years of injustice and rejection at the hands of king Saul. At times fleeing for his life, and living in hiding in caves. Have you ever thought of what might have gone through his mind during those years? 'Was that anointing from Samuel really from God?' 'Has God really chosen me to be king?' 'Why am I having to go through all this?' 'Do I really deserve this after delivering the nation from Goliath and the Philistines?'

If he had had the apostle Paul's writings to hand, he may well have been tempted to ask how on earth this was God 'working all things together for his good!' In some of David's Psalms we get glimpses of the pressures that he was going through, and of how he was feeling. From them we see how he pressed further into his God for help and encouragement. There was no attempt at taking short cuts and helping God out, even when on occasions he had the perfect opportunity, and a 'prophetic' word from his aide, Abishai. (1 Samuel

26:8). David had a settled confidence that what God had determined for him, God in His perfect time would bring to pass. He would not do what king Saul has done, and make some rash opinionated move. We are told that it was not until he was thirty years of age that he was crowned king of all Israel, which meant that he had probably waited around fifteen years for the actual complete fulfilment of God's word to him as a very young man. What powerful lessons of faith can be learnt from David, who in spite of his fallibility, lived his life in heart relationship with his God, who he loved so deeply, and had absolute trust in His word. Even a casual reading of his Psalms constantly affirms this.

There may be times when God calls us to walk with Him by faith, and it may appear from outward circumstances that He has deserted us, or forgotten His word to us. The heavens may seem as brass and the enemy tries to persuade us to give up. It is in those times that we have the opportunity to prove that God is the God that He says He is, and will do all that He has promised. You can come out from these times having discovered yet more of His character and ways, deeper in your knowledge of Him, and further matured as His son.

# Chapter 17

## Always on Duty

~ Without an expectancy to hear the quiet whispers of the Spirit, we are likely to miss the unexpected adventure ~

~ God exists in the eternal 'now' and 'today', and so He is always speaking. It would, therefore, seem that our part is to be always listening! ~

~ Cease from dishonouring God by telling Him what you cannot do, and start to do something ~

We have said much, and illustrated in many ways, the source of faith being in what God is saying, and the necessity of our hearing and moving forward in obedience on what we have heard. I am sure that I have by now made it very evident how important it is to be always expectant to hear what are often quiet whispers from the Lord as we go about our everyday lives, but let us explore the practicalities of this a little further.

I have come across many sincere Christians who believe that God only speaks on Sunday mornings or whenever their church group happens to meet. The rest of their lives are of little interest to their heavenly Father other than that they are living within righteous limits! However, a Christian life that solely centres around the meetings of the church, but is divorced from everyday life, leads to this and many other narrow and distorted ideas. Looking at the life of Jesus we have to conclude that such a concept would have been entirely foreign to Him. Again as we look at the lives of those recorded in the scriptures and the occasions and ways in which they heard the voice of God, we again could not possibly come to this conclusion. Of course God speaks through worship, preaching, the gifts of the Holy Spirit, and indeed as we fellowship together in and around a meeting context. This is an invaluable pursuit, but for even the most ardent meeting attender, this will only be a relatively small percentage of the rest of their lives!

I remember a conversation I had with a lovely elderly lady several years ago. I knew her well, and as a godly person she always had a deep love for Jesus and a ready heart to speak to others about their souls. She was a consistent, but behind the scenes evangelist if there ever was one. At this stage in her life she was clearly finding that some of the teaching she had embraced over the years had become rather at odds with her experiences with the Lord, and her more recent understanding of truth in certain areas. As this had been ongoing for several years and was causing some measure of increasing frustration to her, I asked if she had ever considered finding a fellowship of more like-minded people. Her response was interesting. She told me how that at the age of fourteen, soon after she had become a Christian, God had clearly spoken to her and led her to leave the particular church denomination that she had been with, and move some three miles to a church that taught the Word of God in depth and preached the new birth.

Much later on in her life when she and her husband retired to another part of the country, their new church was of the exactly the same persuasion. However, within this new context she began finding friendship and prayer fellowship with small group of ladies pursuing more of the life of God and of the Holy Spirit. As a result some aspects of her church life were becoming rather a problem to her, although she loved the folks dearly, and always spoke highly of them. She said to me 'You see, God clearly led me to this type of church, (and she named the movement) when I was a girl and that is why I remain here'. The look on her face and the tone of her voice conveyed the permanence that she felt about the situation. She felt she was stuck regardless of the frustrations she was facing. I gently said to her, 'That word that God gave you must now have been over sixty years ago. Do you not think it possible that He may have some further direction for you in terms of your spiritual home, in view of what He has been doing in your life in recent years?' I can still see her stunned face as such a radical idea began to become a possibility to her. Let me say that for her at that time of life moving was probably not an option or the Lord's purpose for her. I am purely using this story to emphasise a point.

I appreciate this may be an extreme example, but it is not as uncommon as many would like to think. This dear lady clearly moved in obedience and faith to the word that God gave her, but never considered that God might speak again on the same matter as her life in Him moved on. I said I knew this lady well – she was my precious mother!

The writer of Psalm 95 makes a poignant appeal set in the context of the unbelief that a previous generation of the children of Israel had exhibited. You also get a graphic picture of how God felt about their deafness, and its results:

> *'Come, let us worship and bow down; Let us kneel before the Lord our Maker. For He is our God, and we are the people of His pasture, and the sheep of His hand.* ***Today, if you would hear His voice,*** *do not harden your hearts, as at Meribah, as in the day of Massah in the wilderness when your fathers tested Me, they tried Me, though they had seen My work. For forty years* ***I loathed that generation, and said they are a people who err in their heart, and they do not know My ways.*** *Therefore I swore in My anger,* ***truly they shall not enter into My rest.'*** Psalm 95:6-11. (Author's emphasis)

I want you to notice the phrase 'Today if you will hear His voice'. The writer of the book of Hebrews in chapters 3 and 4, quotes from this same Psalm three times, each time using that particular phrase, and it is linked with the ability to enter into the rest of God. We as created souls live in a time and space world, and relate to past, present and future, and have our yesterdays, todays, as well as hope for our tomorrows. The eternal God, while of course fully conversant with our time scales, lives in the permanent and unchangeable 'today'. Peter seeks to help by putting it in this rather interesting way:

*'But do not let this one fact escape your notice, beloved, that with the Lord one day is as a thousand years, and a thousand years as one day.'* 2 Peter 3:8

With God it is always 'now' and 'today', and as such He is always speaking. If fact we are told that the very world we live in owes its origin and ongoing existence as a result of the 'word of His (Christ's) power.' (Hebrews 1:2-3). So if He is always speaking, it would seem that our part is to be always listening! I am always amused when I hear Christians say, as many often do when certain situations overtake them, 'I think the Lord is trying to tell me something'. I usually suggest that it is not the Lord who is 'trying' to do anything, as He is always fully able to do what He wills to do, but rather they who may well be audiologically compromised! I find it is us that are trying, maybe in all senses of the word!

Looking at the life of Jesus we see the principle of constantly living daily in the word of God, and showing us the way I believe it is meant to work. For us this is perhaps one of the ultimate challenges to Christian living. Jesus made these following statements:

*'He who does not love Me does not keep My words; and **the word which you hear is not Mine, but the Father's who sent Me.**'* John 14:24

*'Do you not believe that I am in the Father, and the Father is in Me? **The words that I say to you I do not speak on My own initiative,** but the Father abiding in Me does His works.'* John 14:10

*'And I know that His commandment is eternal life; therefore **the things I speak, I speak just as the Father has told Me.**'* John 12:50.

*'I can do **nothing** on My own initiative. As I hear, I judge; and My judgment is just, because **I do not seek My own will, but the will of Him who sent Me.**'* John 5:30

*'Jesus therefore answered and was saying to them, 'Truly, truly, I say to you, **the Son can do nothing of Himself, unless it is something He sees the Father doing;** for whatever the Father does, these things the Son also does in like manner.'* John 5:19. (Author's emphases on all quotes)

Often the question is asked, 'How did Jesus have one hundred percent success in all He said and did?' Every person that came to Him received what they were looking for, be it healing, deliverance, words that had the power to change them, and answers to questions whether sincere and genuine or even attempts at trickery. I suggest the above verses give us the answer. They tell us that Jesus lived in constant fellowship with His Father. Whatever God was saying in any given situation was what Jesus said. Whatever Jesus saw God doing in a given set of circumstances, Jesus did the same. He lived in total and utter dependence on His Father. We have discussed the vital need for closeness and intimacy with the Good Shepherd if we are to hear His voice. Jesus as always is also our example in the matter of His close and constant intimacy with His Father.

Do you mean I have to keep stopping every five, ten, or thirty minutes during my day and have a time of prayer? Of course not, as your employer would rightly be asking some questions concerning your apparent lack of attention to your work. Such ideas spring from a mechanistic form of engaging with God – religion instead of relationship. Jesus clearly had specific regular times of prayer and fellowship with His Father, sometimes lasting all night. There was such a close relationship between the Father, the Son of Man, and the Holy Spirit, and Jesus drew on that resource within Him as He went about His daily business. Whatever circumstances surrounded Jesus day by day, He always had the resources in the Holy Spirit to handle them in line with His Father's will. The people who came to Him, and the various situations were not just chance occurrences, but orchestrated events by God, whose heart was to reach out in kindness and mercy to people in the towns and rural areas as Jesus spread the good news of the kingdom of heaven.

Today we are called and chosen to be followers and disciples of our Master, Jesus, and so the example that He left for us must be the bottom line and goal of our lives too. At this point it is tempting to throw our hands up in the air and say, 'Well, if that is what living by faith is all about, you can count me out. There is no way I can jump a bar at even one tenth of that height!' So we never start, because we decide that the finish is too far out of reach to hope to achieve.
The fact is that had I not written that letter of resignation from my secure employment. Had I not accepted my place at medical school, crazy as it appeared at a natural level. Had I not taken what was that first step of faith into the impossible, and ***begun*** to listen to and trust God, I would not be writing this book, and perhaps I would still be trying to preach theoretical sermons on 'faith' and producing more embarrassing preaching notes, and worse still, even permanent embarrassing CDs instead!

I am convinced that as believers we need to stop telling God what we cannot do, and start taking steps based on what ***He*** says about us, and what ***He*** believes we can achieve, when filled with His life and the power of the Holy Spirit. While we often do not see it this way, it is grossly dishonouring to God to ignore His empowering and argue with what He says we can do. Very often what we are effectively saying is that God has made a mistake as far as I am concerned, and that I know better than He does about me.

If we find ourselves at this place, we desperately need to soak ourselves in all the words of Jesus as He told His disciples of their place and standing in the heart of the Father. John 14 through to chapter 17 is a good passage to start with. For example, Jesus' response to Philip's rather dejected bearing, opens a wonderful and inspiring 'promise box' of possibilities. We have referred to this scripture already, but let us expand our thinking around it even more.

> *'Believe Me that I am in the Father, and the Father in Me; otherwise believe on account of the works themselves. Truly, truly, I say to you,* ***he who believes in Me, the works that I do shall he do also;*** *and greater works than these shall he do; because I go to the Father. And* ***whatever you ask in My name, that will I do, that the Father may be glorified in the Son. If you ask Me anything in My name, I will do it.'*** John 14:12-14. (Author's emphasis)

Greater works than Jesus? Asking anything, in His name, and it will be done? Now in case you should ask me, - No, I cannot think of anything that I have done up to now that could be classed as a 'greater work' than Jesus did, or for that matter have I been in any church context where I have seen that consistently operating. No, I cannot say that everything I have asked the Father to do in the name of Jesus has been effected. Do I sometimes get disappointed by that? Yes. Do I sometimes feel like giving up? Yes. However, I am committed to a journey of faith and full assurance in what God is saying. But I do not let ***that*** make me fold my arms, pout my lips, and declare that scripture does not work! Rather passages like this put fire in my spirit and inspire me to press forward! When things do not appear to work, the one thing I do not do is doubt God. The other thing I will ***not*** do is chat to the devil about the issue – that I have learnt. He and I do not have discussions.

One thing I can say, is that since I have committed myself to living a life of faith, I am seeing more and more of the powerful workings of God, in and through my life than I ever did before. My conviction is that the God of the supernatural and the impossible will increasingly be glorified and manifested in these days, as His people begin to take steps of simple faith, that can develop into strides.

You can learn to fellowship increasingly within your spirit, with the will and purposes of God for every situation, knowing His presence at all times, and learning to hear His words, which may come as whispers throughout your day. You can, because He has sent the promised Holy Spirit to guide you into all truth. (John 17.13.). Remember Jesus said '***all*** truth', which includes the truth concerning His will and purposes for your life.

# CHAPTER 18

# FAITH CAN BE FUN

~ Why do Christians take themselves so seriously when our Father doesn't seem to? ~

~ God might speak in just a whisper, or a soft impression. It's important to catch and obey those too ~

We have been considering some tough issues in our search for understanding the life of faith, so it is time I recounted another story from my medical student days.

During the later three years of the medical course we were required to spend most of our time in hospitals seeing patients. This involved talking to them about their past medical history and their current condition. We were also required with their permission to examine them and check their medical notes. Then there was the need to examine the results of various tests and x-rays. This was all to enable us to develop the skills required to diagnose and treat patients of our own after we had qualified. While there was a fair amount of classroom learning that had to be done in the form of lectures, reading and practical laboratory work, these later years were mostly spent in the hospital environment on hospital wards and operating theatres at various specialist and general hospitals around the university city, and in some cases other outlying towns. The number of students had to fit the number of patients available, as while book learning is important, much of medicine is learnt by talking to, and examining patients, while following their treatment and progress. We were expected to join the consultants' daily ward rounds, when there would be up to a group of six medical students following as a retinue, and desperately hoping the consultant would not ask some searching question in front of the patient and thus expose our ignorance. It seemed to us that the consultants always had the knack of asking us questions that we never had the answer to – most embarrassing! Later, as qualified doctors we would teach medical students in this way ourselves, and have a little inner smile as we remembered our own trauma on these occasions!

Part of our assessments during this period consisted of what were called clinical examinations, when patients with different conditions were asked if they would be happy to be student examination 'guinea pigs'. We then were asked to talk to the patient about their condition, how it all started, details of their symptoms, the degree of pain if any, and the site of their problem so that we obtained a clear picture of the start and the progression of their disease. We then had to examine them. All this was usually with the examiner present, normally an experienced senior doctor, to listen and observe your procedures. The patient was of course sworn to secrecy about their diagnosis and treatment. Occasionally one or another would take pity on our ordeal and drop out a clue or two! You can imagine that this was a harassing ordeal, made worse by having a case in which you had not the slightest idea what was wrong with the patient even after your interrogation and examination!

I recall one of these examinations, which on this occasion was in the subject of paediatrics, concerning diseases in children. Children always make interesting patients for examinations, as sometimes they are too young to talk or answer your questions, or refuse point blank to speak even when they can. Others will tell you a whole load of rubbish purely for the fun of it. Yet others howl incessantly throughout the whole procedure. So these hazards can add another entire dimension to your trauma!

As always, I committed these events to the Lord for His strength, wisdom and peace, which in reality was usually something less spiritual and more like 'O God, I need Solomon's wisdom right now, please!'

As I was coming to the end my final revision the evening prior to the examination, I did ask the Lord if there was anything else that I should refer to, or that would be advantageous for me to look at. I thought I felt the Lord say to me 'liver disease'. It was really what I call a 'cobwebby' word – faint, fine, whispy, a soft impression. I remember thinking – why liver disease, that is pretty rare in children. I am very unlikely to get a case tomorrow in the examination. I could not recall there being a case in the hospital, as I had been around all the wards over the preceding few days. As students we were always trying to assess which patient might be used for our clinical examinations, although I am sure our examiners would easily remember doing the same themselves during their student days! I think this was one of the first times that I had had this type of word from the Lord – it was more of an impression. Maybe like Elijah experienced when he finally heard the very quiet 'sound of a gentle blowing' that was the voice of God, after a massive mountain rending wind, earthquake and volcanic eruption. (1 Kings 19:11-13.)

It is late, I need sleep to be alert for tomorrow, and was that really God anyway. I doubt if there will be that sort of a case tomorrow. On and on went my clever rational thought processes. But then I thought, what is the point of asking the question in the first place, if I am not going to listen to the Lord. I must be prepared to hear Him, however He chooses to speak to me. I reopened my paediatric textbook and turned to the chapter on liver disease and quickly realised I knew far too little about the subject in respect of children. I had better spend some time correcting this deficiency.

I presented myself for the examination the following morning, and my first two examination cases went reasonably, but I did not feel I had done as well as I would have liked. I was then ushered into the room for my third and final case. The room was quite dark and I was presented with a baby, a few months old lying quietly in a cot. There was no sign of the mother, so I was not going to get any leads from that source. The temptation is not to disturb the child unnecessarily – let sleeping babies lie! – but I remembered my tutors repeated instruction – 'Always examine the patient in the best light possible or you will miss something.' I asked for the light to be put on in the room. I guess that was worth a few marks anyway!

There before me lay a lovely little Asian girl who clearly is small for her age, obviously failing to thrive. As I examined her eyes, there was the tell tale yellow pigment in her schlera (the whites of the eyes), and I knew immediately the child almost certainly had jaundice. Top of the list for the likely cause had to be – liver disease! I examined the child and detected an enlarged liver. Now I was ninety nine percent certain she had liver disease. At this point the examiner asked me what I had found, and we began to discuss abnormal liver conditions in the newborn in a general way, and then in this child in particular. The examiner gave me details of the tests that had been done on the child and asked me to comment on the findings. I recall that I really got into the subject and found I was enjoying myself immensely, with the examiner and I having a really warm and friendly discussion on the subject. This was not usually how it went – normally more like ice cold polar bear versus terrified mouse! I had never known an examination quite like it, where I was actually relishing the whole affair. Right at the end of the interview the examiner casually asked if I would like to suggest a possible diagnosis for the child in question, almost as an after-thought. Now you may think that strange, as surely that was the essential purpose of the test. However, the examiner was far more concerned with the student's ability to assemble the facts, examine the patient, and form a list of the most likely causes of the illness. At that level you were not failed for missing the exact diagnosis.

While waiting to come into the examination, I had been reading about a very rare metabolic liver condition in the newborn which I had never even heard of prior to that, let alone had ever come across in my clinical training. This child seemed to fit this condition perfectly, and so without batting an eyelid I said, 'My diagnosis would be Galactose-1-Phosphate disease due to enzyme block.' As I write it down now it still sounds impressive! My examiner's look of surprise told me I had made a hit. This was a diagnosis at paediatric consultant level, not 4th year medical student. I had passed my paediatric clinical with flying colours. Father and I had quite a praise party on the drive home! Incidentally I found out that they had 'imported' this little girl from another hospital just for the clinical examination – I am glad God rumbled them, and that I listened to Him and responded! Incidentally, I have never seen a similar case with this condition since then to this day. It is pretty rare!

I have learned that it is wise to be ready and able to hear what initially seem to be passing impressions, to check with the Lord further, and then to act on them. I wish I could say that I always have done this since that time, but on several occasions, particularly when listening in on a conversation, I have sensed what I thought was that quiet voice of the Spirit but not said or done anything in response. Later I have learnt that events have taken place that were exactly what I had picked up at that time, and might have been averted if I had had the boldness to speak out.

I hope you enjoyed the story of the examination that turned out to be fun, when it could have been a monumental disaster! I still chuckle today about the great time the Lord and I, and my examiner had on that occasion.

# Chapter 19

# Partners in Faith

~ God requires me to co-labour with Him, declaring His creative word into situations, so that they yield to Christ's rule and government ~

~ I am responsible before God to act on those things that I ***do*** understand, not on those that as yet I do not! ~

During the years that God has been leading and teaching me in the life of faith, I have been the student, and He rightly has been the Master, and of course this is how it always will be. However, in more recent years, as my understanding and confidence in Him has grown, I have come to realise that I am required to operate in my sphere of influence where He has placed me, and declare the creative word of God into situations, so that they yield to Christ's rule and government.

The scriptures make it quite clear that the word of God creates the life of God within us. Jesus when being tempted by Satan in the wilderness quoted the following old testament scripture: '***Man shall not live on bread alone, but on every word that proceeds out of the mouth of God.***' Matthew 4:4 Again, John in quoting Jesus says '***....the words that I have spoken to you are spirit and life.***' John 6:63.

It is not just that God speaks to me and I obey, like a mechanical robot. No, it is a living word that even of itself imparts His very life into me. It carries inherent within it the creative life of God, and when spoken out from me, has the dynamic authority to change situations. Jesus many times chastened His disciples for their lack of faith through not using their God given authority in this way. He obviously had expected them to speak to the elements and still the storm on the lake. The fact that they did not, revealed more about ***them*** and their lack of faith than anything else. It has occurred to me that when reading and commenting on the incident, we usually make far more of Jesus' power over the storm, and like the disciples say 'Wow!', when we should probably be saying 'Wow' about the panic and ineptitude of the disciples, as we go on to apply the lesson to ourselves.

The prophet Habakkuk makes an interesting observation: '***But the righteous will live by (his) faith***' Hab.2:4. This scripture is then quoted on three separate occasions in the new testament. In Romans 1:17, the context is that of my faith in the power of the gospel. In Galations 3:11, it is to do with freedom from the law that faith provides. Finally, in Hebrews 10:38, it is concerning my walking out with endurance my life in God, through that faith that is living on the inside of me. Faith becomes a source of life ***within*** us, and must become a fountain of life ***out from*** us.

My conviction is that relatively few believers have grasped the truth of the fact that we are not on this planet to pass the time away just attending meetings until Jesus returns. We have a clear mandate to bring His kingdom rule to earth. Is not that the very mandate that Adam and Eve were given but failed to do? Was it not the mandate that passed to the nation of Israel to enact – to make the surrounding pagan nations see what just and righteous government was all about? Has not that mandate now been fully restored to the church through the death and resurrection of Christ? Why on earth should Jesus teach His followers to pray and request God for 'Your kingdom to come, Your will to be done on earth as it is in heaven' if that were not to be effected in this present age? Is not this exactly what Jesus did all the time? Whenever He met sickness, death or demons, He commanded the situation in heaven to come to earth, there and then. Because there is no sickness, death or demons in heaven, when He commanded the will of heaven to invade earth, those things had to go, every time. I trust we would all agree that the situation that exists in heaven is always fully in line with the will of God. Thus when heaven is called on to invade earth, the situation here has to yield to that divine will!

I remember many years ago sitting in a prayer meeting and becoming acutely aware for the first time of how many prayers were offered up which included the words 'help me' and 'help us', and I began to listen more closely as to what those people praying were asking help for. In fact I began privately to call them 'help me' prayers. In many cases it was for something that God had already promised that He had done! For example, the prayer 'help me to be more loving' sounds spiritual at first hearing. However, Paul tells us the that: ***'the love of God has been poured out within our hearts through the Holy Spirit'*** (Rom.5:5.), and he repeats much the same truth in Ephesians 3:17-19, and in 2 Thessalonians. 3:5. As sons and daughters of God through the life of the Holy Spirit, God ***has*** poured His love into us, so should we not be receiving the impact of that word into our hearts, believing God in faith that this is the truth of His life within us already, thanking Him for such a privilege, and actually looking for a clear opportunity to express that divine love to someone? I have heard well intentioned folks pray these sort of prayers for years, yet they never seemed to change. 'Help us to die to ourselves'. No folks, just die - after all, that was what your baptism was declaring, - and start living out the resurrection life of Jesus, drawing on the constant filling of the Holy Spirit. Paul tells us to 'reckon ***ourselves*** dead' not plead with God to kill us! If we truly have been 'crucified with Christ' then He already has! So why is this corpse still asking to be helped to die?

We so often parade our imagined weaknesses in prayer, hiding behind them, and moaning to God about them. Really this ends up as just an excuse for not taking His word over us with assurance and conviction, believing in what He has made us to be, and obeying what He has called us to do. To pray opposite to God's word, is an affront to Him. It is saying, 'I really do not believe I am who You say I am, so please will You help me to be different.' If you think it through, I expect you can anticipate the answer you are likely to get! Having been delivered from the kingdom of darkness, into the kingdom of God, brought into intimacy with the King through the power of the cross and the resurrection, and filled with the Holy Spirit, we are now sent out into the world to declare His glory and excellencies. His word becomes our offensive sword with which ***we*** speak and declare what ***God*** is declaring into situations. Similarly, that same word, on which we put our full reliance and act out our obedience, becomes our defensive shield which protects us from all harm. We become invincible! (Ephesians 6:16-17).

Please do not misunderstand me. There are times when it is right and needful to call on the Lord for His help and deliverance, and I am sure that most believers will have had to do that on more than one occasion, and can give testimony to His answer. I certainly have, and that is absolutely correct. You will recall from my story the time when through my mother's scribbled note there came the promise of God to hold my hand and help me. I guess deep down the night before I received that promise, this was the cry of my heart, which Father in His grace and kindness heard. But having received it, I then had to put my complete confidence in that promise in every situation thereafter. It did not have a 'sell by' date on it! I did not go on praying 'O God, help me, by helping me, and help me helpfully to be helped!

Again I remind you that we are called to be co-labourers (1 Cor.3:9) with Christ, right here and now, on this planet earth. Just as Jesus worked, yoked inseparably to His Father as we have already discussed, we too are called to work in the same way, bringing the Father's will to earth, as we live out our everyday lives. That is the reality of what it means to live and walk by faith. In other words it is a journey lived stepping out daily on God's word. What a privilege.

The little discourse from Jesus on faith, following the cursing of the fig tree is one that is frequently raised. People will say to me, 'Well, I prayed for something in accordance with what Jesus said and it did not happen.' The inference is that because it did not happen then this is proof that faith obviously does not work. In fact it is a clear teaching on the whole matter of co-labouring with God in our walk of faith. To me it is the high watermark for all those who would seek out this path.

> *And Jesus answered saying to them, 'Have faith in God. Truly I say to you, whoever says to this mountain, Be taken up and cast into the sea, and does not doubt in his heart, but believes that what he says is going to happen, it shall be granted him. Therefore I say to you, all things for which you pray and ask, believe that you have received them, and they shall be granted you.'* Mark 11:22-24

The essential elements here are:

*1:* Have the God-kind of faith (See Chapter 5 on this verse). Get that 'measure of faith' working that God has given you. Remember also in 1 Corinthians 12:9, Paul tells us that faith is one of the spiritual gifts that we have been given.

*2:* Speak out the creative word to the obstacle, that God has spoken first into you.

*3:* You now have the '*underlying immovable rock-like structure that turns hope into complete certainty, and gives concrete and irrefutable proof that what we are unable to perceive with our natural senses, is in fact real and fully in existence.'*

*4:* You can then receive what you have believed for, and declare it as done. (Recall my story in Chapter 8 about the special wood stain. I had 'received' it before it was in my physical hand).

These verses, rather than being intimidating, are to me the disciple's goal in living the Christian life, working with the Father as a royal son, to bring His will and government to a very needy world. I would be the last to attempt to put forward clever explanations as to why people who have claimed these verses over the years for impossible 'mountain moving' situations, have not seen the mountain as yet moved. I would also be the last to comment on the level of faith of the petitioners concerned. I am in no place to analyse such matters, and instructed not to even try to judge. I too have had times where it has not worked for me, in situations where I believed I had heard God. There are many things in my walk with God that even after all the many years He has led me I still do not understand. However, I know I am responsible before God to act on those things that I ***do*** understand, which are numerous, and I refuse to let the enemy make me stumble and use the things I ***do not*** understand to question the goodness and integrity of my Father.

Maybe when I am living in complete obedience to what He has already revealed, He may open up some further revelation into other mysteries and issues that at present defy my knowledge! In spite of all that, this is what Jesus taught His disciples one day as they walked with Him. It is clear that Peter and John following the powerful anointing of the Holy Spirit at Pentecost brought dramatic healing to the lame man in Acts 3, and the Acts catalogues and refers to big 'mountains' getting shifted as we have discussed in chapter 12. Those first disciples had moved from being students to practitioners. That is also my quest – I trust it will always be yours.

## CHAPTER 20

# THE ANTITHESIS OF FAITH

~ Unbelief will follow fear, and unbelief will always chain you to inaction ~

~ As soon as I refuse to pursue His will and purposes, He ceases to be Lord of my life, and I serve only my self interests ~

~ Repeated failure to hear and obey God's voice produces a hard heart, which then becomes deaf and impervious to any further words ~

As with all issues surrounding our life in Christ things are invariably black or white. While our humanity longs to 'sit on the fence' and keep all options open, with God this is never on offer! Over the years I have noticed in society an increasing culture of indecisiveness. Ask many folks today, particularly younger generations, a question that requires a decision, and you rarely receive a clear answer. I am often asking people if they will get involved in some certain event or serving in some way, and I frequently get the reply, 'Well it all depends'. I have now learnt to ask 'Well, what does it depend on? to which I get the retort, 'Well, I don't know really'! What I am being told is 'I do not want to make my mind up because something better may turn up that I will wish I had gone for'. Of course, the standard Christian response is often 'I will have to pray about it' which roughly translated means 'I cannot think of a good reason right now how I can get out of this, but this answer will get you off my back!' You know perfectly well in ninety-five percent of instances they have no intention of praying about the issue, or of coming back to you with a positive answer. This same prevarication easily spills over into the way we live our Christian lives.

We cannot get away with that in our life with God. He requires an answer, an action, a 'yes' or a 'no'. 'I will go halves with You on that Lord' will not work, as to the Lord that equates with 'no' and is a denial of His Lordship anyway. Jesus made it very plain that we cannot serve two masters. We either love one and hate the other or vice versa. The fact is that if He is truly 'Lord' of our lives, then the answer 'no' to any request He might make of us is completely out of bounds. 'Lord' means He is the loving boss of my life. As soon as I refuse to pursue His will and purposes, He ceases to be Lord of my life, and I serve only my self interests.

I have already made reference to the statement that can sometimes be heard by Christians concerning a person who is involved in Christian work that does not receive a regular salary or income, as someone who 'lives by faith'. When I hear that phrase, the question always rises up in me, which I sometimes voice is: 'Well, what do the rest of us live by? - unbelief!' There is no middle ground. We either live by faith founded in God or unbelief which is founded in ourselves, fuelled generously by Satan.

Unbelief is the exact opposite of faith. We have seen from Romans 10:17, that ***'...faith comes from hearing the Word of Christ'.*** The antithesis of this could be stated as: 'unbelief comes by not listening out for, or not listening to, and not obeying, the Word of Christ.' While this is not scripture itself, scripture upholds the truth of this as we shall discover.

Unbelief is simply a failure to action the constantly spoken fresh word of God into my life. We have many avoidance mechanisms to justify our absence or lack of faith. Many people never give any time whatsoever, to hear God speak to them. Their lives are so full of noise and clutter - sometimes 'church' noise and clutter - that they would not hear a spiritual jet aircraft at ten feet away. They may protest that they are avidly 'serving God' with every spare moment, and in terms of Christian works they may well be. Yet Jesus our perfect example, took heaps of time out to spend with His Father, resulting in always doing and saying the same as His Father. The result? One hundred percent success. Not really quantum physics is it?

Others have gained the idea that you have to be very 'spiritual' to hear God and live by faith, so they disqualify themselves. It is just for the 'platform ministries' to live and demonstrate to an awed congregation. I am sorry, you cannot hide behind that. Remember

God speaks to sheep, not university professors – unless they happen to be His sheep too. Remember, living by faith is God's requirement for ***every*** believer ***all*** the time, that is if we are to please Him.

Someone has made the point that fear is the converse to faith, and I think there is a lot of truth in that. Faith is the conviction of that which God has said will certainly happen and is as yet unseen. Faith rests in God's resources. Fear is the conviction of that which Satan has said will or might happen, and with our agreement is supported by clear evidence all around us and in our everyday natural experience. Fear feeds on the lack and limitations of human resources. Much, if not all, of our unbelief finds its source in fear, and fear paralyses us from any action that lies outside what we have come to understand as 'normal'.

From my own observation and experience I have found that faith is like a powerful force enabling God's will and purposes to invade and change the natural realm around us. Conversely, unbelief is an opposing force that will lock up situations and render ineffective what faith would have opened. I never read the account of Jesus coming to His home town as recorded in Mark, without being staggered at the effect the town's people's unbelief had, even on the ability of Jesus to perform the miraculous works of the kingdom of heaven among them. Even Jesus was astonished at their reactions:

> *'And He (Jesus) went out from there, and He came into His home town; and His disciples followed Him. And when the Sabbath had come, He began to teach in the synagogue; and the many listeners were astonished, saying, 'Where did this man get these things, and what is this wisdom given to Him, and such miracles as these performed by His hands? Is not this the carpenter, the son of Mary, and brother of James, and Joses, and Judas, and Simon? Are not His sisters here with us?' And they took offense at Him. And Jesus said to*

*them, 'A prophet is not without honour except in his home town and among his own relatives and in his own household.' And* ***He could do no miracle there except that He laid His hands upon a few sick people and healed them. And He wondered at their unbelief.*** *And He was going around the villages teaching.'* Mark 6:1-6. (Author's emphasis & parenthesis)

Another classic illustration of the paralysing effect of unbelief, was that experienced by the children of Israel after God had so miraculously delivered them from the bondage of Egypt in order to bring them into their promised inheritance. It was a promised land 'flowing with milk and honey'. A land they could call their own provided by God at no expense to themselves. Twelve spies, a man from each tribe, was sent to reconnoitre Canaan and bring back a report. When they returned after about six weeks, they all confirmed that the land did indeed 'flow with milk and honey'. As proof they brought back a single cluster of grapes that took two men to carry it. However, they also had observed that there were giants as well as other nations in the land who lived in strong massively fortified cities. Ten of the spies assessed the situation and reported that any thought of conquering these inhabitants was futile. Israel did not stand a chance against such enemy occupiers. Caleb, followed by Joshua, did not deny the facts that they also had observed, but came to a completely opposite conclusion based on exactly the same facts.

*'And Joshua the son of Nun and Caleb the son of Jephunneh, of those who had spied out the land, tore their clothes; and they spoke to all the congregation of the sons of Israel, saying, 'The land which we passed through to spy out is an exceedingly good land. If the Lord is pleased with us, then He will bring us into this land, and give it to us-- a land which flows with milk and honey. Only do not rebel against the Lord; and do not fear the people of the land, for they shall be our prey. Their protection has been removed from them, and*

*the Lord is with us; do not fear them.' But all the congregation said to stone them with stones. Then the glory of the Lord appeared in the tent of meeting to all the sons of Israel.'* Numbers 14:6-10

Caleb and Joshua believed the promises of God, rather than what they observed with their natural eyes. In their spirits they saw all these enemies completely defeated before the armies of the Lord of Hosts. They perceived that God had already removed their military strength from them. They speak out against fear. Their rallying cry was 'Let us go and get them for breakfast! God will bring us into the land.'

*'But the men who had gone up with him said, 'We are not able to go up against the people, for they are too strong for us.' So they gave out to the sons of Israel a bad report of the land which they had spied out, saying, 'The land through which we have gone, in spying it out, is a land that devours its inhabitants; and all the people whom we saw in it are men of great size. 'There also we saw the Nephilim (the sons of Anak are part of the Nephilim); and* ***we became like grasshoppers in our own sight, and so we were in their sight.'*** Numbers 13:31-33. (Author's emphasis)

Please pay attention to the words of unbelief. 'It is a land that devours its settlers'. How did they know that? They had not even tried to settle there yet. 'The cities are walled up to heaven.' – what impossible nonsense. Listen further to the language of unbelief: 'We became grasshoppers in our own eyes, and thus we became in their sight.' Do you now see here illustrated the power of unbelief? It is like looking at yourself through a pair of binoculars the wrong way round – you become the size of a grasshopper, and start telling yourself that is what you are! Then you look at your enemy with the binoculars the correct way, and conclude he is an undefeatable giant, and you begin to tell yourself that also. But notice the effect it had on their enemies. Their negative confession about themselves, founded in fear, made their enemies feel twenty feet tall. 'Now you come to mention it you Israelites, you are just a heap of tiny grasshoppers, and my, we really are the greatest!' Exactly the same situation prevailed with King Saul and with young David when faced with Goliath. The same giant uttering the same words, but resulting in entirely ***opposite*** perspectives. Not slightly different.

The massed voices of unbelief prevailed over the two voices of faith, and a whole generation, probably at a conservative estimate about one and a half million people, were consigned to forty years of wandering in a desert until their deaths. Only those under the age of twenty at that time would ever see the promised land, except for Caleb, who God declared had a 'different spirit and has followed me fully' (Numbers 14:24), and Joshua.

In chapter 17 I referred to chapters 3 and 4 of the letter to the Hebrews. In the context of what we are looking at here, it is well worth a careful study of these chapters. The writer is referring directly to the period in the history of Israel that we have just been discussing. The main point I would highlight from them is that the repeated failure to hear and obey the voice of God will cause the development of a heart that becomes hard and impervious to any further word from God, and thus failure to inherit God's promises. We are given a timely encouragement to faith:

> *'Let us therefore be diligent to enter that rest, lest anyone fall through following the same example of disobedience.'*
> Hebrews 4:11

These chapters relate an old covenant story in a 'better' new covenant setting!

I realise that I have laboured the negative issue of unbelief in this chapter, but I have sought to underline and highlight its deceptive power. In my early Christian experience I can look back with some regret to such paucity of spiritual life and lack of vigour that unbelief brought to me. I have witnessed far too many unbelieving 'believers' living on the wrong side of God's promises for most, if not all, of their lives. This must sadden the heart of God, as well as being such a waste of a Christian life of fulfilment. Our thinking must be constantly renewed, through repentance, to receive the word into the good soil of our prepared hearts, and with His power that works mightily within us, live by faith. Remember, even if you realise that you have spent far too much of your life in unbelief, it is 'Today, if you will hear His voice', and your life of faith can begin. God never locks us into our history, only you can allow that to happen.

The enemy will do everything to challenge faith, because He knows there is nothing that can prevail against a believer living by it. Faith causes devastation to his kingdom. It is unassailable. It is the reason why he came to Adam and Eve as he did in the garden of Eden, and immediately called into question the word of God to Eve, causing her disobedience and the fall of humankind. Instead of a settled faith on what God had said, Satan's voice sowed doubt and fear that perhaps God was holding something back from them after all. Let us never believe the same lie. God is constant and eternal in His goodness, and His passionate love for us. Never let outward circumstances rob you of that unchangeable truth.

# CHAPTER 21

# THE LAUGH OF FAITH

~ With tears streaming down my face, I blurted out through bouts of mirth, 'This is the most crazy financial decision we have ever made, especially as we haven't got a bean to pay for it! ~

This is a final story about how there can arise within us laughter, even when the circumstances should make us cry! This again is also a personal record of what God will do in increasingly impossible circumstances, if we make room for Him through our obedience.

Around the time that our fourth child was due to leave primary school for his secondary education, both my wife and I began, quite separately, to sense that the Lord was wanting us to send him to the private cathedral school in the town in which we lived. I initially struggled with this whole concept, as our three older children had all attended state schools, and I had never ever considered it as an option, mainly on the basis of cost, having five children, and partly on the basis of principle. However as the time drew nearer, we increasingly sensed that this was the Lord's direction.

We took the first steps and obtained the details from the school. The fees alone made my eyes water and rendered the whole project appear dead in the water, unless he could obtain a scholarship to cover them. We applied for the scholarship, only to be informed that they were solely music scholarships which usually required a certain level of expertise in two instruments, although if he were very proficient in one, he could still be considered. He had done very well in piano examinations, so we decided to enter him for the entrance examination and the scholarship. He passed the entrance examination with flying colours, but his music was not of the standard they were able to accept. No scholarship was available. We chatted with our other children as to how they would feel about their younger brother being singled out for this rather special treatment, and they assured us that such a move would not cause them any problems, especially if this was what God wanted.

It is interesting to see how and when God chooses His moments. At that very time we were financially heading for the rocks. For the very first time in my life, I was in the red at the bank, and I mean that literally. We were really struggling to make ends meet. We had moved home to another area which had been costly, and the church we were leading at that time was quite small and unable to support us very much at that stage, although we were very grateful for the generosity that they were able to afford us. I only had part-time medical work, as I needed to give some quality time to see the church grow.

Into this mix the Lord served us a curved ball. We are sensing His voice and purpose in respect of our son. He now has a place available in the school. Our expenditure is already more than our income, and there is no future foreseeable way to change this. We therefore cannot finance the venture. While we know God is not short of the cash to pay the fees, we have no indication of how this will be. An accountant looking at the proposition would quickly inform us of our stupidity in the light of such impossible and irresolvable circumstances.

We left the decision of taking up the place at the school until the night before the final deadline, hoping that 'something would turn up'. It did not, and we were to go away on that final Friday morning to stay with friends for the weekend. We decided to sleep on it and hope for a dream or vision, or some other dramatic divine manifestation, such as an angel, or earthquake that would clinch things for us. My wife and I had totally undisturbed dreamless sleep – not the slightest glimpse of even the tip of an angel's wing or vibration in the house foundations! We both therefore had to resort to the simple approach, as I have described elsewhere. We get into a place of quiet, rest and in peace before the Lord. 'Lord what are we to do, take the place or not take the place', and move out on the answer that He drops into our spirits. Both of us independently had the same answer – 'Take the place.' A quick note to the school headmaster was written, and as we drove past the school on the way to our weekend away, we dropped it into the school office by hand.

I will never forget the scene in our car as we drove up the hill away from the school and out from the city. We both quite spontaneously burst into fits of uncontrollable laughter. We did not plan it, or try to manufacture it. We were not putting on a brave face. In fact I guess we should have been silent with the apprehension of what we had just committed ourselves to. With tears streaming down my face, I blurted out through bouts of mirth, 'This must be the laugh of faith, that I have heard about, because it is the most crazy financial decision we have ever made, especially as we do not have a single penny to pay for it.' We returned from our weekend, to find a cheque that was obviously already in the post, quite unknown to us even as we made the decision. It was completely out of the blue from an entirely unexpected source, covering at least thirty percent of the first term's fees. We knew that this was God's seal and first-fruits of what He would do.

Within only a very few weeks of these events, the Lord made it clear that I was to resign from my part-time medical work. What an excellent idea, seeing our personal financial situation was tending to worsen, now with a son committed to private education for the next seven years, and the church not able to support us any more than they were. Things could not get much more crazy! This must be God, so I handed in my notice!

Twenty four hours following my final day in the job, I had a telephone call from a lady asking for me. She went on to explain that she worked at a centre that assessed and treated children who had suffered neurological damage or defects from birth, or as a result of later trauma or disease. She stated that she had met me recently in her own general practitioner's surgery were she had understood that I was a locum doctor. Would I be free to cover their medical requirements for a while as their previous doctor had left suddenly without notice and they were in a serious predicament? When I managed to get a word in, I informed her that I had never in my life been in the surgery that she had mentioned, neither was I a locum doctor, and I certainly had no recollection of meeting her. I asked her how she had managed to obtain my telephone number, and she said, 'Oh that was easy, I just looked up Dr. Stephen Wood in the medical directory, and there was your name, address and telephone number.' I was completely nonplussed, especially when she kept on insisting that she had met me and clearly remembered my name. I could not help coming quickly to the conclusion that God was in all this somewhere – the whole story seemed as equally crazy as my positive response to the Lord to leave my previous job. I was not exactly inexperienced in these 'happenings' that defied all logic and natural explanation. I guess I was rather like the disciples when Jesus came walking on the water to them – 'It must be the Lord!' My, my, how sharp we are!

My recent employment circumstances of course had made it possible for me to follow up her request, and I agreed to visit the centre and discuss their medical requirements. I was quite naturally very intrigued as to how she had heard of me, especially as previously I had had some experience in neurological problems during my hospital work. When I arrived at the centre for my initial visit I proved not to be the person that they were expecting, although our names roughly tallied. They were completely baffled as to what had happened, but as I appeared to exactly fit the role they were desperate to fill, they were just very grateful about the 'mistake'. It was some time later that I told the director of the centre how I had come to be involved there, and who had orchestrated the whole affair! God was certainly not the centre of his world, and his quizzical look said more than words, but for once he was speechless.

I ended up being the medical consultant to this centre for some fifteen years, becoming very involved for the majority of that time in helping and seeing the centre develop and expand its range of treatment approaches. My close involvement with the families of these children proved particularly rewarding. As I remained the centre's external medical consultant, I was able to work my hours and days around my church leadership requirements as well as their requirements, and also able to charge appropriate fees for my services. Within twenty four hours of my signing away what income I was earning at that time, the Lord provided more than enough to cover seven years of my son's schooling fees, and our family needs.

The amazing twist to the story is that some six months after becoming involved with this centre, I learned the answer to the puzzle of my mistaken identity which proved convoluted and full of several 'co-incidences' that I could not start to outline them here. Let me just say they were almost beyond the bounds of credibility. No one will ever convince me that faith cannot shift mountains.

People have asked me if we ever thought why God wanted only our one son to go to a private rather than the local state school, which incidentally was a good school. Yes, we have thought about this many times over the years, but apart from hazarding some guesses, we have not the slightest idea, but one thing we ***do*** know, this was just another fun test along the journey of walking by faith with our heavenly Father.

# EPILOGUE

We have come to the end of our journey, and I trust you have benefitted from the account of God's faithfulness through all these experiences. More than that, I believe that this account will be the inspiration for many readers, to begin to experience their heavenly Father in a fresh and deeper way.

As I meet and talk with Christians, I find that many of them appear to have little expectation that God might use them in any significant way. Yet I am convinced that God has plans and intentions for us all, that stretch beyond our wildest dreams.
God spoke to His people Israel through the prophet Jeremiah at a time when things were very bleak in the life of the nation:

> *'For I know the plans that I have for you,' declares the Lord, 'plans for welfare and not calamity to give you a future and a hope.'* Jeremiah 29:11

These were people under the old covenant, and the letter to the Hebrews tells us that through Jesus, a better covenant, that had better promises attached to it, is now the portion of the people of God through faith. (Hebrews 8:6).

We can live our whole lives reading from scripture the wonderful examples of men and women of faith, and be inspired from their stories, and rightly so. We can do the same when reading and hearing the stories of men and women of more recent times. We can study in detail all the references in scripture to faith, and the different thoughts and shades of opinion that have been propounded over the years. Yet personally never take one single practical step of faith for ourselves.

Some may take that initial step of repentance from their life in sin, and believe the word of God that provides His loving provision of forgiveness and salvation in the cross of His Son Jesus Christ. Yet they may never take another step of faith into those paths which God has prepared for them. They never become true disciples - which is a practical and ongoing learning process. It is like so many of the young children that I worked with in medicine, who sadly, for various reasons, were never able to stand on their feet and walk for themselves. Exploration and fresh exciting discoveries were denied them. Likewise it can be like that in spiritual development, which is equally sad. Being birthed into the kingdom, but failing to grow any further. I am convinced that the intent of God's precious truth is to bring us into an increasing intimacy with, and revelation of, Him. To know His will for our lives, which we are called to pursue and obey. As I have said elsewhere, truth, that does not lead us into a living experience of Him, through failure to outwork it, will only serve to make us religious, such as it did the Pharisees in Jesus' day. For the most part, they knew the scriptures, yet sadly completely missed the One of whom they spoke. What a great privilege it is to know we are called to live by faith, and to experience the joy and wonder of working together with Him, every day of our lives. However, let us never forget that all the glory goes back to Him, for it is by His grace alone that we have been saved and called into His family. May God richly bless you, and enable you to get out of the boat!

o o o o o o o o o o o o o o o o o o o

**Contact the author at:**
**reception@bathcitychurch.org.uk**

Lightning Source UK Ltd.
Milton Keynes UK
26 October 2010

161938UK00001B/19/P